Democracy, Justice,
and the
Welfare State

Julie Anne White

Democracy, Justice, and the Welfare State

Reconstructing Public Care

The Pennsylvania State University Press
University Park, Pennsylvania

Library of Congress Cataloging-in-Publication Data

White, Julie Anne, 1965–
   Democracy, justice, and the welfare state : reconstructing public care / Julie
Anne White.

        p.   cm.
   Includes bibliographical references and index.
   ISBN 0-271-02002-4 (cloth : alk. paper)
   ISBN 0-271-02003-2 (pbk. : alk. paper)
   1. Welfare state.   2. Democracy.   3. Justice.   4. Paternalism.   5. Public
welfare—New York (State)—New York Case studies.   I. Title.
   JC479 .W48 2000
   330.12'6—dc21   99-34788
                                                                                  CIP

It is the policy of The Pennsylvania State University Press to use acid-free paper for
the first printing of all clothbound books. Publications on uncoated stock satisfy
the minimum requirements of American National Standard for Information
Sciences—Permanence of Paper for Printed Library Materials, ANSI Z39I.48-1992.

Contents

Preface and Acknowledgments

This book attempts to outline a framework for practices of public care consistent with our democratic commitments. I think it takes some important preliminary steps in that direction. My work draws on the contributions of many others and is the better for it. Having said that, the process of revising what is here and moving beyond it is an ongoing one.

This project is grounded in an analysis of two case studies of social service collaboration. I believe that this close interrogation of the actual practices of care illuminates both the important contributions and the limitations of previous work on care. But in the interest of honesty I must acknowledge that the project design unfolded as a consequence of fortuitous coincidence. I was lucky enough to find a niche with the Center on the Organization and Restructuring of Schools at the Wisconsin Center for Education Research. I am grateful to Gary Wehlage, the assistant director, for taking me on as both a student and a research assistant. Working with Gary provided the access to Annie E. Casey's New Futures programs, and when the Beacons looked like a helpful comparative case study, he came up with the funds to support site visits. As a mentor, he consistently reminded me that my work should be accessible to policymakers and practitioners. And though I often found it challenging to weave together an account of theory and practice that made the threads connecting them visible, I hope there are places here where that happens. If there are, Gary can take much of the credit for that.

The theoretical work here reflects conversations with many others. Joan Tronto's work *Moral Boundaries* was a formative influence on this project. I thank Joan for her patience in working through two drafts of this manuscript. I'm not sure I have answered the hardest questions she posed, but I am sure the work was improved by her comments. Sanford Thatcher, editor and director at Penn State Press, was a pleasure to work with. I have appreciated his commitment to feminist scholarship both as an author and a reader.

Murray Edelman, Bernard Yack, and Marion Smiley influenced the construction of this project in critical ways. Murray's work continues to shape the way I approach my own and his encouragement early in my graduate study is what kept me going. Bernie was supportive through what I'm sure seemed to both of us like a long process of writing! My deepest thanks go to Marion Smiley. She saw this project through from several false starts to the finish. Her careful reading and insightful responses were critical to moving the project forward and I continue to learn from her work as both a scholar and a teacher. Marion and Bernie effectively fostered a working group of students writing in the field of political theory. Since leaving graduate school we all have new colleagues but this group remains an important system of support for which I am grateful. To Greg Streich and Lisa Nelson I owe particular thanks for all their contributions to my thinking on the subject of democratic care. Greg generously gave time he didn't have to let me interrogate him about his work on deliberative democracy. Lisa Nelson talked through this project from beginning to end and was a supportive critic throughout.

I have had rare good luck where colleagues are concerned; here at Ohio University, too, their influence and support has been invaluable. DeLysa Burnier's work on program evaluation helped me think through the institutional implications of my argument for a democratic politics of care. John Gilliom's study of welfare reform and surveillance reinforces and then moves beyond much of what I argue here. John was both a mentor and a friend and I thank him for both. Taka Suzuki's intellectual energy has been inspiring and often contagious and one cannot want more in a colleague than that. Yet I owe Taka a second debt as well, for he patiently helped me through what was ultimately the most anxiety-producing part of this project: dealing with my computer. On all counts, I am grateful. My colleagues in philosophy and women's studies also helped shape this work. Celeste Friend's work on trust is an important alternative to the account I began with and she pushed me to think through my position. Toward the conclusion of this project conversations with Christopher Zurn were particularly helpful. Chris tried to dissuade me from too facile a critique of the justice tradition. I think it will take another volume to fully respond to his concerns but his comments may have motivated me to write it! I have appreciated Alden Waitt for both her comprehensive knowledge of feminist work and her sense of humor, and her ability to discern when I needed the later rather than the former. A friend, indeed.

Others contributed in less direct but no less important ways. My good friends Alisa Rosenthal and Joel Shoemaker had the patience to work through ideas even at their most formative stage. I respect Joel and Alisa as intellectuals and as activists and their comments on this project were help-fully informed by both sets of commitments.

Amy, Jeff, Andrew, and Logan Blake provided get-away space, though for many years this project came with me and ended up strewn across their dining room table for weeks at a time. They were patient and supportive through it all and I am indebted to them for that. My father's commitment to his own academic work is a model for me, and both my parents, James and Muriel White, supported and sacrificed for my education — an incom-parable gift. My partner, Joseph Hazelbaker, has put up with the narcis-sism that is often (and ironically in the case of a book on care) involved in writing and remained a generous spirit throughout. Joe still believes that we might be able to change the world; on good days he even persuades me. That, too, is an incomparable gift.

This book is dedicated to my mother. She taught me most of what I know about compassion and care, not only as my mother but as a nurse and, most recently, a Peace Corps volunteer. While I'm not sure she would call herself a feminist, I am sure she practices much of what I value in feminism every day. I admire her strength.

1

Introduction:
The American Welfare State

Exploring Our Ambivalence
Toward Public Care

Why should those of us concerned with the making of politics and policy care about "care"? Of what relevance is care as a category of political analysis? What does the institutional context for "good care" look like? Is there such a thing as "bad care"?

These questions are difficult in part because implicit within them is a challenge to the traditional conception of care itself. In commonsense usage, as well as in much of the theoretical work, care is conceptualized as a private virtue, a natural inclination. The model for care is most often taken to be the family, particularly the relationship between mother and child. Given such a conceptualization of care, making "caring" public policy, or developing an *institutional* context that facilitates the work of care, may seem an impossible if not outright contradictory project.

I begin this project by arguing that in the context of the modern welfare state the question of how care should be organized is of public and not merely private, political and not merely psychological, significance. Yet the actual organization of care in the public sphere suggests that while the division of labor that positioned care as private is challenged in the modern welfare state, other aspects of its association with the family remain uncontested. Specifically, I argue that care in the context of the modern welfare state tends to replicate the authority relationships of a traditional family and that therefore it produces paternalistic practices of care in the public sphere. My task here is to suggest an alternative model of care that challenges this conception of authority in favor of a democratic politics of care.

Professional Versus Political Care

As much work within feminist theory has illustrated, the traditional conception of the place of "care" as a private practice is in large part a function of modern, particularly liberal understandings of the political self as the autonomous self and the contractarian state as the sum of these selves.[1] Care as a practice of meeting needs implies a challenge to liberalism's vision of the public self as the autonomous self, where the ideal of autonomy is equated with self-sufficiency. This claim to self-sufficiency is critical to the liberal understanding of freedom: one can make freely considered, rational judgments only when one is free from dependence on others. Autonomy frees individuals from the dependency, contingency, and vulnerability that might interfere with such judgments.[2] In this sense, autonomy transcends necessity. While liberalism has always had to acknowledge some relationships of care as indispensable, liberals have largely argued that the needs of political subjects should be addressed prior to their participation in politics in order for that participation to be free and rational.[3] In this

1. See Butler [1978] 1995; Hirschmann 1992; Mitchell 1998; Pateman 1989; Tronto 1993.
2. Sevenhuijsen 1998, 139. For more on the relationship between liberal understandings of freedom and autonomy, see Hirschmann 1996 and Mitchell 1998.
3. Although Arendt herself is not easily classified as a liberal, her vision of freedom shares much in common with the liberal vision of freedom that I articulate here. Bernard Yack offers the following analysis in his discussion of Arendt: "Arendt reinterprets Aristotle's understanding of man's political nature in the light of a modern philosophy of freedom that opposes our human qualities to our natural qualities. . . . Any influence, such as poverty, that 'puts men

sense, while care in the private sphere has always been necessary to support the public sphere (not least because such care was necessary to creating those autonomous selves, to creating good citizens), it is only with the relatively recent rise of the welfare state that care has been considered a public practice. In traditional contract theory, the neglect of care as a public value had been premised on the acceptance of a construction of separate public and private spheres and a corresponding division of labor that positioned care as a private activity. Moreover, the public/private split worked to maintain this division of labor as gendered, and the opposition between public and private came to coincide with the opposition between male and female — between the political and the natural, the rational and the emotional.[4]

Yet, as Linda Nicholson (1993, 92) has argued, this series of associations is not itself natural or inevitable. Rather, such a conception of public and private as bounded spheres of activity is a product of modern, particularly liberal forms of social organization. These forms of social organization have their roots in the early modern period in the West with the rise of the nuclear family and the nation-state. Large-scale public institutions such as the modern state must abstract from the needs of particular persons and govern through the creation of universal laws. Alternatively, emotional support and nurturance are the task of the family.[5] Situating our common understandings of care against a broader historical account of the evolution of public and private spheres helps to explain how it came to be positioned outside the public sphere in the first place. In addition, historicizing the location of care and tracing its shifts also suggests that in placing care on the state's agenda (in its commitment to the public provision of care), the modern welfare state challenges this basic division of labor.

This challenge is an ambivalent one, however. For while the division of labor across public and private spheres is altered, the association of care with natural (and therefore familial and private) rather than political activity remains in other ways largely unchallenged. In the modern welfare state, where the concern for the welfare or care of others has become a

---

under the absolute dictates of their bodies, that is, under the absolute dictates of necessity' represents for her a 'dehumanizing force.' For Arendt, political activity is an achievement of human freedom against our natural inclination. . . . The language Arendt imposes on Aristotle's understanding of political community makes our political character something we assert *against* human nature" (Yack 1992, 71).

4. See Pateman 1989; Gatens 1991; Bubeck 1995.

5. Blum 1982, 287–88, cited in Nicholson 1986, 164.

matter of public policy, care has evolved as a set of professional rather than political practices, as a matter of social policy designed by experts rather than a contested practice (Fraser 1990). I argue that welfare policy as a public practice of caring retains care's depoliticized (here, professional rather than political) status as a holdover from its original association with the private, "natural" sphere. The authority of the provider of care came to be naturalized in the public sphere just as parental, particularly paternal authority had been in the private sphere, both assuming authority in relation to a class of dependents. In light of this, authority in relationship to those designated "needy" has been conceived as legitimately paternalistic. In the context of liberal democratic commitments that presume the independence and autonomy of actors as prerequisite to full participation in the public sphere, such dependence is incompatible with full citizenship.[6]

Marion Smiley (1989) has suggested that the problem of paternalism in the modern welfare state is best understood in terms of the question "How can we regulate these activities without treating mature adults as if they were mentally incompetent children?" She argues that if we want to avoid treating citizens paternalistically in this sense, we will need to place paternalism in its appropriate political context. This move, Smiley continues, would open up the possibility of democratizing the process through which we create our private and public spheres. I have already suggested that the welfare state challenges the traditional division of labor across private and public spheres. But in our current system, such processes of redefinition tend to be bureaucratic rather than democratic.

Criticisms of bureaucratic professionalism abound, and it is not my intent to add to this literature. There are others far better suited to that task.[7] But the tension between the political and the professional that many commentators have noted is of particular importance to understanding how the process of designating the "needy" and defining their needs unfolds in the practices of the contemporary American welfare state. Historically, the Progressives were a key force pushing for the expansion of the welfare state and particularly for the expansion of public education.[8] This expan-

6. For example, those who are recipients of public care are often subjects of state surveillance, of invasions of privacy that would be viewed as unlawful were the subjects not receiving welfare benefits. See Gilliom 1998.
7. For two particularly good accounts, see Code 1991, especially chapter 7, and Ferguson 1984.
8. For two preeminent accounts of Progressivism in public education, see Cremin 1961, and Tyack and Hansot 1982. For a more critical perspective, see Katz 1977.

sion was accompanied by a move to professionalize control of the schools and settlement houses, where professionalization was quite explicitly contrasted with democratic control. The reform movement reflected the antipathy, widespread among Progressives in social work and social policy as well as in education, for "the sordid world of politics" (Bowles and Gintis 1976, 187). In this context lie the origins of the "caring professions."[9] A public commitment to care evolved as a set of professional rather than democratic practices, entrusted to experts rather than citizens.

Given the opposition between the professional and the political supposed by this model of reform, it is hardly surprising that public "care" continues to be properly thought the domain of expertise rather than the domain of politics even in the contemporary welfare state. In this context, the "needs" that care addresses tend to be framed in a process of expert assessment through the mapping of individual or community pathologies, which are addressed through the implementation of categorical programs—the entire process of which seems to be considered more a science than a politics.

Defining Needs

In making this argument, I use the term *modern welfare state* to refer to interventions in the form of public social provision aimed at modifying the play of social or market forces and justified by reference to the "welfare" of recipients. The term *welfare state,* however, implies an assumption that must be proved: that the state actually promotes the welfare of its citizens through such social policy. As we shall see in the following chapter, my analysis of current practices in the provision of social services prompts some skepticism about this assumption.

In the context of current institutional practices, the authority to define what counts as welfare, to determine what recipients need, belongs to a class of professionals; and this authority is justified by reference both to the specialized knowledge of professionals and to the lack of competence

9. I have suggested that much about the traditional division of labor across public and private spheres remains unchallenged in the modern welfare state. One aspect of this division of labor that remains unchallenged is the association of women with the work of care. Thus women are vastly overrepresented (and underpaid) in the "caring professions." See Bubeck 1995.

on the part of dependents. Such specialized knowledge doubtless has its place in informed decision making. As Lorraine Code suggests,

> There is nothing contentious about the assertion that there are close connections among knowledge, expertise and authority. People commonly assume that knowledge is the basis of expertise and that expertise confers authority on its possessors. A person of recognized expertise is usually in a position to have his (and sometimes her) pronouncements respected and to be consulted as an authority when expert advice is required. (Code 1991, 181)

She continues:

> This state of affairs is simply part of the division of intellectual labor essential to the smooth functioning of complex epistemic communities. The advantages of the division clearly outweigh the disadvantages, for no one could acquire all of the specialized knowledge a person would need in order never to be reliant on someone else's expertise. (182)

It is undoubtedly the case, as Code suggests, that only a small percentage of our knowledge is first person, experiential knowledge.[10] Reliance on expert others is often unavoidable. But it is important to see the way in which the institutional setting of expertise shapes the terrain of debate. To return to the case of professionalized public care, a traditional bureaucratic structure often produces deference to experts without much direct democratic accountability to clients. When there are conflicts over welfare programs, these conflicts tend to be framed as technical or implementation problems for the welfare system. This is perhaps clearest in the debate about allocation of funds. Efficiency becomes the key word, with little explicit discussion of which ends are worth efficiently achieving. By framing conflicts in this way, we skirt a directly political consideration of a very difficult question: What is welfare?

To illustrate this tendency and the dilemmas that flow from it, I employ two case studies of social service collaboration. Both represent attempts to reorganize public care at either the municipal or county level through a process of social service collaboration. Advocates of collaboration were

---

10. For an excellent account of the politics of "second person" knowledge, see Virginia Held's *Rights and Goods* (1984), especially chapter 5, "The Grounds for Social Trust."

committed to improving social service programs serving youth and families designated "at risk." In the first case, New Futures, advocates emphasized that this required getting the "right people" — that is, those who currently control services — to the table. Their project was to discuss how such services could be delivered more efficiently. A critical focus of this collaborative effort was eliminating redundancy of services through tightening inter-institutional linkages. Yet my study suggests that in the process of negotiating the gaps between institutions of social service, the critical gap between service providers and the recipients themselves remains largely unchallenged.

At the outset, collaboration advocates framed social service collaboration as a technical problem. Given this, the "right people" for the job of collaboration were those with technical expertise. My analysis of this collaborative effort suggests that questions such as "Who participates in the discussion of what the 'needy' need?" are critical. I ask specifically: How does the identity of participants affect policy design? What is the source of the assumed consensus on *what* is needed? How does framing the problems of welfare policy as "technical problems" influence who has authority in deciding how to deal with them?

The case studies allow me to address such questions in the context of actual practices of public care. My evaluation of New Futures' collaborative effort illustrates some of the inadequacies of current practices of care as they are commonly organized. Specifically, the case study demonstrates a critical disparity between the needs of recipients as defined by professionals and the needs as articulated by recipients themselves and their advocates. I argue that a more adequate version of care requires an explicitly political understanding of the process of interpreting needs — a move away from associations of need as professionally assessable to considerations of need as public, political, and most important, contested.

Where care is recognized as a political rather than a professional practice, it becomes necessary to talk about the process of determining needs as political — actually as a process of interpreting needs rather than expertly assessing them. And once we have said that needs are interpreted (actively) rather than merely assessed or discovered expertly (where need would be taken to be an artifact for discovery), it becomes critical to ask who (actively) participates in the process of interpreting and why. That is, what are the criteria for participation in this process? And on the basis of this criteria, who is included and who is excluded from the process?

Building on the work of Nancy Fraser, I reconceptualize "needs" as constructed by, and responded to, within the context of a network of social and political relations (Fraser 1989, 145). Within this network are multiple understandings of need; that is, meeting needs is not only about implementation problems within the current system but also about differing, often incompatible understandings of need itself. The recognition that need is contested and that professional assessment often cloaks this is fundamental to exploring potential reconstructions of the process of interpreting and meeting needs, reconstructions of public care. Framing the issue of public social provision in terms of technical or implementation problems reinforces the power of professionals to control the debate by framing the issues as technical in *opposition* to political. The qualification for participation in the process of defining needs is membership in "an expert specialized public." Those whose needs are in question are "positioned as potential recipients of predefined services rather than as agents involved in interpreting their needs" (Fraser 1989, 174).

The Character of Care

I do not simply attribute the place of professionals in defining needs to the culture of a "credential society" or a kind of cult of expertise. These terms imply that the same rules of expertise and judgment apply to all, for that is the very nature of our understanding of professionalism. Yet it is relevant to this discussion that in our public discourse, "needs" are uniquely the property of a class of "dependents" — of the "needy" as opposed to those who are normal, self-sufficient, able alone to care for themselves. The identification of this group as dependent, as opposed to the norm of self-sufficiency, legitimates paternalistic relationships of authority in the form of expertise. The logic of this justification for paternalistic care is instructive. Note that one is either self-sufficient and therefore does not require care, or, alternatively, one is dependent and deviantly so and thus requires not only care but paternalistic authority. If paternalism is not justified, neither is public care.

Fraser and Gordon (1994) note that in the contemporary welfare state, dependency and neediness are often treated as though they are aspects of individual character; needs become *properties* of individuals rather than the *products* of social relations, and as such they set themselves outside politics. Thus even *dependency,* a term that appears necessarily to entail the relationship between dependent and depended upon, seems in common usage to have become an identifier of a quality or character of individual persons.

To illustrate this, we might examine the popular discourse surrounding contemporary welfare reform. Welfare dependency has been depicted as a "social malady," a societal "pathology." Yet if it is a disease of the body politic, the diagnosis has been that the "pathology is concentrated among the minority dominated urban underclass" (Whitman 1992, 36). What makes welfare dependency so threatening here is the sense that these poor are not the deserving poor; they are the able-bodied of less-than-noble character. Perhaps, some concede, the system has even contributed to this character deficiency by creating incentives for illegitimacy, crime, illiteracy, and more poverty (Gingrich 1994, 65). But the policy response is clear. While the welfare dependent certainly needs a job, what she needs even more is a sense of personal responsibility. Hence the Personal Responsibility Act: "Our Contract with America will change this destructive social behavior by requiring welfare recipients to take personal responsibility for the decisions they make," and by "requiring that welfare beneficiaries work so they can develop the pride and self-sufficiency that comes from holding a productive job" (Gingrich 1994, 65). To string the clichés together: we have a welfare state that has created a "culture of poverty," which results in a "cycle of dependency." This cycle can be broken only by "ending welfare as we know it."

The critique of dependency and its juxtaposition with self-sufficiency has been an ongoing feature of the debate about welfare policy, even among advocates of welfare programs. Take, for example, the Johnson administration's War on Poverty. Though these programs are much criticized by contemporary welfare reform advocates, the rhetoric surrounding the Economic Opportunity Act is in some important ways eerily similar to that in the "Contract with America." Gareth Davies (1992, 205) has argued that Johnson's program, like the New Deal tradition that preceded it, owed much to its congruence with popular individualism, an individualism premised on self-sufficiency and the belief that the poor should engineer their own paths to affluence. He adds, "Among supporters of the Economic Opportunity Act, antipathy to the spectre of dependency was uniform" (219). Davies argues that the logic of equal opportunity rather than equal reward had as its corollary "a deep hostility to welfare dependency which Johnson shared and was eager to tap" (218). This faith that individual motivation combined with equal opportunity would produce self-sufficiency is one that Johnson shared with FDR. For Roosevelt too argued that "to dole out relief . . . is to administer a narcotic, a subtle destroyer of the human spirit"; he fully expected the able-bodied to take advantage of public work programs.[11]

In the American context, the assumption that dependency is cause and consequence of character failings seems to be shared by both advocates and critics of the welfare state. But while the emphasis on the self-made man may be excessive in this context, theses on American exceptionalism aside, self-sufficiency is a tenet of western liberalism broadly conceived. Selma Sevenhuijsen (1998, 28) comments on the Dutch context:

> In this respect I have always found the objective of government policy of ensuring that every citizen should in principle be able to look after themselves — an aim which was laid down in Dutch emancipation policies in the 1980's — to be paradoxical. This norm of self-sufficiency and the related view of human nature assumes each citizen to be a detached individual whose aim is autonomous behavior, who needs nobody and who recognizes dependency and vulnerability only in others. It means that care figures in politics as a handicap, as a burden or as a "necessary evil." (Zwinkels 1990; Tronto 1993; Werkman 1994)

Sevenhuijsen's concern that we only recognize others as needy is a very real one. Yet in the context of the contemporary welfare state, it is most often the case that when we identify someone as needy, we are not actually suggesting that their character lends itself to excessive neediness. Rather, at least where adults are concerned, it is by virtue of the fact that their needs are met by the state rather than the family that the label "needy" is applied. It is revealing that when we talk about the problem of dependency, the image that comes to mind is not that of the college student whose parents financially provide for her needs or the stay-at-home mother whose partner is the breadwinner. These may be relationships of dependency, but they are not typically viewed as problematic. By contrast, the stay-at-home mother who depends on public assistance rather than a domestic breadwinner to meet her needs has come to define the problem of

---

11. Schlesinger quoted in Davies 1992, 210. A 1994 Roper survey conducted among residents of New York State suggests that the belief that welfare encourages irresponsibility is still strong among Americans; 78 percent of those surveyed said they believed welfare led to a "spiritual and moral disintegration." See Mitchell 1998, 37.

dependency. But it is not clear why the relationship of dependency on the state should say any more about her character than the relationship of the more traditional housewife to her partner says about hers. While the work of stay-at-home moms is still vastly undervalued, we do not typically think of them as exemplifying a crisis in "personal responsibility." I am suggesting that relationships of dependency are a much more integral part of the human condition than we are often willing to recognize.[12] Such dependency is cloaked by the citizenship ideal of self-sufficiency. As Sevenhuijsen continues, "The ideal of abstract autonomy in fact overlooks what it is that makes care an element of the human condition, i.e., the recognition that all people are vulnerable, dependent and finite, and that we all have to find ways of dealing with this in our daily existence and in the values which guide our individual and collective behavior" (1998, 28). If Sevenhuijsen is correct, and I believe she is, this suggests that despite our commonplace associations with the terms *needy* and *dependent* as naming character attributes, they can only make sense politically if we take them to refer to a particular relationship to the state embodied in the practices of public care. In a real sense, these practices create the "needy" as a class. They are not simply addressing a prior dependency; they are institutionalizing it. Locating the problem of the "needy" in an institutional set of arrangements, in relationship to institutional issues of authority, we can argue that an alternative set of institutional arrangements could serve as a remedy.

The Problem with Paternalism

Defining dependency as a quality of the individual character justifies state paternalism as it has traditionally been conceived. In its familiar version, usually derivative of Mill's work in *On Liberty,* paternalism is defined as state intervention in the lives of self-regarding individuals for the welfare of the subjects of intervention (Regan 1974; Rothman 1981; Sartorius 1983). In this version, there seem to be two possible responses to the paternalism critique. The first is that the "cared for" is not, in fact, rationally

12. Both Mitchell (1998, chap. 2) and Sevenhuijsen (1998, chap. 5) argue that in order to properly value care, we must begin with an account of individuals not as autonomous, but as vulnerable. I shall develop the connections between their analysis of vulnerability and my own concerns regarding dependency in Chapter 6.

self-regarding, and therefore paternalism is justified. Young children are the most obvious example. But among adults, "self-regarding" is translated into "economically self-sufficient." Thus, those who cannot support themselves financially, those who are therefore understood as dependent, are also considered legitimate subjects of professional intervention. The alternative response to the paternalism critique is that the "cared for" is rationally self-regarding, and state paternalism as an act of caring is misplaced; the cared for should be left to him- or herself. If paternalism is not justified, neither is care.

Yet, the paternalism critique so formulated is unhelpful both conceptually and politically. Conceptually, it is often very difficult to distinguish between activities that are self-regarding and those that are other-regarding. Mill attempts the following distinction:

> The maxims are, first, that the individual is not accountable to society for his actions in so far as these concern no one but himself. Advice, instruction, persuasion and avoidance by other people, if thought necessary by them for their own good, are the only measures by which society can justifiably express its dislike or disapprobation of his conduct. Secondly, that for such actions as are prejudicial to the interests of others, the individual is accountable and may be subjected either to social or to legal punishment if society is of opinion that the one or the other is requisite for its protection. (Mill [1859] 1956, 14)

Intervention is almost never justified in activities that are self-regarding. In the few cases where Mill argues that intervention in self-regarding activities is justified, he does so by reasoning that nonintervention threatens the individual's future freedom; that is, his or her future right to nonintervention in self-regarding activity. While such an exception seems coherent by utilitarian logic, it may not be politically so, for its political coherence rests on a distinction between self- and other-regarding actions that has become notoriously problematic as a guide for making policy.[13]

Where paternalism is understood as the tension between state interven-

13. Even Mill himself recognizes the difficulty in drawing this distinction. He attempts a clarification: "The distinction here pointed out between the part of a person's life which concerns only himself and that which concerns others, many persons will refuse to admit. How (it may be asked) can any part of the conduct of a member of society be a matter of indifference to the other members?" He responds by admitting the difficulty of drawing the distinction between self- and other-regarding, but insisting on it all the same. See Mill [1859] 1956, 97–100.

tion and self-regarding individuals, all actions of the state become unhelpfully problematic. In our own political practices, we lean heavily to interpreting most action of individuals as self-regarding, and the tension between self- and other-regarding has largely been dealt with through the establishment of a space for, and limits to, individual rights.[14] It is in the context of these commitments and against the backdrop of a liberal political culture that paternalism becomes such a forceful criticism. For paternalism names the failure to respect the capacity and right of the self-regarding individual to define his or her own good.

But again, this forceful criticism is unhelpful as a guide for action. Because the distinction between self- and other-regarding is messy at best, we may find ourselves disagreeing even about when paternalism has *occurred* (that is, whether the motive for intervention was a benevolent interest in protecting the other from him- or herself, which we would call paternalism, or whether it was justified intervention in other-regarding activities, in which case we would call it not paternalism but regulation) as well as when it is *justified* (that is, given that the motive for intervention was benevolent interest in the future freedom of another, whether such intervention was in this particular case warranted or not). Thus, the paternalism critique as it is currently formulated seems problematic. Where, then, does this leave us with respect to the practices of care?

I opened with a series of questions: "Why should we care about 'care'? Of what relevance is care as a category of political analysis? What does the institutional context for 'good care' look like? Is there such a thing as 'bad care'?" First, I have tried to suggest that the commitment to welfare in the modern welfare state makes care a relevant issue for political analysis. Second, I have briefly suggested that the institutional context of public welfare policy tends to produce paternalistic practices of care; that is, care that assumes the dependence of its subjects. Perhaps we would not go so far as to call this "bad care," but we would probably be willing to acknowledge that such practices are in tension with other commitments of a liberal democratic political culture.

For example, for those who see themselves as committed liberals, paternalism represents a form of domination with which to be concerned. The dependence relationship implicit in paternalism violates the commitment most obviously to autonomy. For where paternalism is justified as inter-

14. For two accounts of rights that take account of feminist concerns regarding their uses and limitations in the American context, see Mary Ann Glendon's *Rights Talk: The Impoverishment of Political Discourse* (1991), and Elizabeth Kiss's "Alchemy or Fool's Gold? Assessing Feminist Doubts About Rights," in *Reconstructing Political Theory* (1997).

vention for the dependent's own good, it violates the liberal commitment to allow each individual to define for him- or herself what constitutes his or her own good. But in framing paternalism in this way, as an issue of justice, as a kind of violation of the rights of autonomous individuals, what place is left for care at all? There is a sense in which a strong commitment to autonomy as derivative of individualism may be antithetical to valuing care. Nonpaternalism based in a strong commitment to autonomy as self-sufficiency would seem to produce a strong skepticism of any form of collective responsibility or responsiveness at all. In short, to rid ourselves of paternalism might well mean to rid ourselves of politics altogether.[15]

Yet there is a set of alternative objections that we might raise to paternalistic practices of care. I think it is helpful at this point to separate "liberal" from "democracy" in thinking about these objections. I have suggested that care evolves in the contemporary institutional structure of the American welfare state as a practice largely controlled by professionals. In light of this, I have just suggested that these practices might be criticized as a violation of individual autonomy, at least as it is often understood by liberals.[16] But such practices might also be criticized with respect to the democratic commitment to equal participation. On this formulation, we might imagine that the alternative to paternalistic practices of care is a more democratic process of participation — specifically in the course of defining needs. Thus, to rid ourselves of paternalism might well be to move toward a more democratic process of needs interpretation premised on equal participation in defining needs. This seems a more helpful way to conceptualize the paternalism critique if it is to serve as a guide to practice, particularly the practices of public care.

I will elaborate a reconceptualization of paternalism along these lines. If we understand paternalism as the process of speaking for others in the

15. Many others have noted that politics is threatened in liberalism. For a nice overview, see Bonnie Honig's *Political Theory and the Displacement of Politics* (1993), especially her chapter on Rawls. Also see Benjamin Barber's *Strong Democracy* (1984) for an account of liberal democracy as "thin democracy." I will address this theme in greater detail in Chapter 7.

16. We need not, some argue, throw the proverbial baby out with the bath water. While dominant understandings of autonomy as self-sufficiency are problematic, autonomy can be reconstructed so as to be conceptually and politically compatible with care. Jane Flax (1978) has argued that we might reconstruct autonomy so that it is no longer understood as incompatible with relationships of nurturance. Mitchell (1998, chap. 5) too argues that autonomy is a "worthwhile value" but that our politics must begin by presuming vulnerability and attend to reducing or eliminating it in order to achieve autonomy.

course of defining needs, we may be able to criticize domination in the practices of care without simultaneously threatening the prospect of collective responsibility for care. In addition, having suggested that needs are interpreted in a political process, we have made problematic the role of expert knowledge in the process of needs assessment. The challenge to such specialized publics has political ramifications. Qualifications for speaking in this process of defining needs may come to be understood in terms of the practical knowledge gained from direct experience; hence, the criteria for recognizing and respecting one's authority to speak may shift. Thus, to be in a position to know something about needs is in part determined by the experience of being in need in a particular way. These moves seem necessary to the development of a democratic politics of care.

The Project Summarized

In what follows, I develop both a conceptual and institutional framework for a democratic politics of care. Because I am interested in institutional questions, I begin by examining the practices of public care within their actual institutional context. I present two case studies that illustrate some of the problems of care in practice. I then move on to examine other conceptual work on "the ethic of care" to provide a critical lens through which to view the case studies. I argue that much of the conceptual work is inadequately attentive to the problems and politics of needs interpretation evidenced in the case studies. In particular, these studies seem to demonstrate some of the problems of professional needs assessment with respect to both process and outcome. How might such problems be addressed? I begin with a discussion of work that examines the distinctions between justice and care and that then attempts to map out their proper roles and places in relation to one another. I ask whether supplementing care with justice might serve as a corrective to the problems reflected in the case study. Ultimately, I conclude that at least in many contemporary formulations, modifying the practices of care in accordance with the standards of justice produces incoherent conceptual alternatives unhelpful as guides to practice.

I move on to explore work that insists that care has always been a required if unacknowledged component of our conception of justice. Are the problems with care demonstrated in the analysis of practices really best understood as a failure to fully realize our commitments to justice? Specifically, would adopting a different model of distributive justice necessarily produce better care? In light of the primacy of issues of identity, community, and trust revealed in the case study, I am skeptical. I come to the conclusion that where justice is associated with impartiality, it is difficult to make caring just.

My analysis of this conceptual work, taken together with the cases, suggests the importance of an alternative epistemology that moves away from impartiality as the basis for legitimate knowledge and the foundation for legitimate authority.[17] As the case studies demonstrate, it is such expert "impartiality" that legitimates the paternalistic practices of care that we now have: experts speaking for others in the course of defining needs. Leaving aside the question of whether experts get needs right (and there is evidence that they often do not), this process tends to produce both distrust and resentment.

Rather than understanding the problems of care in the modern American welfare state as problems of injustice, I argue that we might better understand them as problems of paternalism. The corrective, then, is not "just care" or justice as we have traditionally conceived it, but rather it is nonpaternalistic care, the institutionalization of a democratic politics of care.

Such a democratic politics of care would move away from impartiality in favor of direct and partial engagement with the context of need as the basis for authority. With this move, the question "Who counts as having the knowledge relevant to defining needs?" is answered quite differently. As a consequence, the politics of needs interpretation would need to be democratized. This, I argue, is a necessary if not sufficient step in the direction of a democratic politics of care.

In this chapter I have tried to suggest that in the context of the contemporary American welfare state, our commitment to public care is an ambivalent one, deriving from a concern that public care requires public dependency. Such dependency is seen as a threat to the primacy of liberal individualism understood in terms of self-sufficiency and autonomy. In the following chapter we will examine the consequences of this ambivalence for the actual practices of care.

17. See also Walker (1989) for an account of the relationship between alternative epistemologies and feminist ethics.

2

Caring for Those "At Risk"

A case study of social policy illustrates some of the problems of "care" in practice. The Casey Foundation's New Futures programs demonstrate three key points. First, the delivery of "care" in the current institutional context tends to evolve as a paternalistic practice, assuming a permanent class of caregivers and a subordinate class of dependents, and privileging the expertise of caregivers in the process of defining needs. Second, despite the fact that the project was designed to improve services for youth and families designated "at risk"[1] and ultimately to improve outcomes, it failed to do so. I attribute this failure to an inadequate understanding on the part of providers of needs of the "target" population, those receiving care.

1. I want to be clear in using the expression "designated 'at risk'" that the term *at risk* is a social designation employed by one group, usually care providers, to designate another, usually recipients of care.

Third, a more adequate understanding of needs would have facilitated better policy, but such an understanding required participation of the target population in the process of interpreting needs, and, despite an explicit commitment to participation at the outset, this participation never happened. New Futures thus illustrates a paternalistic model of care. The final section briefly compares New Futures to an alternative effort at collaboration, the Beacons programs in New York City, which I argue illustrate the potential of a model based on more mutual practices of care.

The New Futures case study, which serves as the primary focus of this chapter, illustrates well what Nancy Fraser has called "expert needs discourse." Fraser describes this classification of needs talk as a primary feature of the modern welfare state:

> They [expert needs discourses] are closely connected with institutions of knowledge production and utilization and they include qualitative and especially quantitative social science discourses generated in universities and "think tanks" . . . administrative discourses circulated in various agencies of the social state; and therapeutic discourses circulated in public and private medical and social service agencies.
>
> As the term suggests, expert discourses tend to be restricted to specialized publics. Thus, they are associated with professional class formation, institution building and social "problem solving." . . . And expert discourses become the bridge discourses linking loosely organized social movements with the social state.
>
> Because of this bridge role, the rhetoric of expert needs discourses tends to be administrative. These discourses consist in a series of rewriting operations procedures for translating politicized needs into administrable needs. Typically, the politicized need is redefined as the correlate of a bureaucratically administrable satisfaction, a "social service."
>
> . . . As a result of these expert redefinitions, the people whose needs are in question are repositioned. They become individual "cases" rather than members of social groups or participants in political movements. In addition, they are rendered passive, positioned as potential recipients of predefined services rather than as agents involved in interpreting their needs and shaping their life conditions. (Fraser 1989, 174)

It is exactly this translation of "politicized needs"—needs that are located within a system of social relationships of which domination is one characteristic—into "administrable needs"—needs that appear to be uncontested, determined, or defined in a process of expert consensus—that prevents what Fraser calls a more "oppositional" needs discourse from taking place. "By virtue of this administrative rhetoric, expert needs discourses too, tend to be depoliticizing," she writes (1989, 174). An examination of the design of New Futures as well as of the practices that unfolded during the course of the project illustrates this expert needs discourse and its consequences for public care. By contrast, the Beacons projects in New York suggest the possibility of a more "oppositional" form of needs talk when needs are politicized "from below."

The New Futures Project

My interest in the problem of paternalism arose in the course of evaluating programs for youth and families designated "at risk." These programs were ambitious attempts to improve the opportunities available to at-risk families. Despite this ambition and commitment, there can be little doubt that this program was unsuccessful by its own criteria for success: to positively influence rates of dropout, teen pregnancy, and teen unemployment. There are detailed records of New Futures programs in five cities over a five-year period to document this.[2] My analysis is an attempt to offer some insight into why, despite investment of substantial resources, both financial and technical, New Futures organizations proved to be inadequate to the tasks they had set for themselves. The focus of the second part of my analysis demonstrates that in accepting a largely technical understanding of both the problem and the solution, the project left unchallenged the institutionalization of a class of caregivers (usually justified in terms of expertise) and a class of recipients of care, a division of labor that reinforced a paternalistic model of care. By defining "the problem" to be addressed in terms of "inefficiency and redundancy" in services, and "the solution" as institutional collaboration, New Futures avoided more offen-

2. For a complete account of the data collected in each city over the five-year period, see *New Futures: Results of a Groundbreaking Social Experiment in Five Cities,* authored and published by the Center for the Study of Social Policy, March 1995.

sive explanations like the "culture of poverty" arguments often used to explain the genesis of "at risk" populations. But as organizations, New Futures collaborative projects largely accepted and then replicated internally the current division of labor in the practices of care — privileging the voices of experts and professionals in defining the needs of those designated "at risk." Establishing nonpaternalistic practices was not a goal of the Casey Foundation or of New Futures organizations in any one city. But avoiding paternalism may be a critical component in moving toward the outcomes to which New Futures is committed.

I do not intend to offer a detailed account of the New Futures Program here. Rather, I rely on Foundation literature, my own interview work, and interviews completed by other evaluators to tell a part of the project's story.[3] While New Futures had some important successes in facilitating interinstitutional linkages and coordinating leadership of social services, I am interested in exploring the relationship between this collaborative form and the outcome goals New Futures set for itself. This story is a familiar one in the context of public care.

History: Five Cities, Five Years

Approximately nine years ago, the Annie E. Casey Foundation, a nonprofit organization committed to improving educational opportunities for disadvantaged youth, began "New Futures," the largest of their projects involving five medium-sized cities with large "at risk" populations. Sites included Savannah, Georgia; Little Rock, Arkansas; Pittsburgh, Pennsylvania; Dayton, Ohio; and Bridgeport, Connecticut. The indicators used to define "at risk" populations included high rates of school retention and suspension, teen pregnancy, and post-high-school unemployment. In order

3. Interview work was conducted in the course of site visits in 1994 and 1995. Interviews conducted in the process of evaluating New Futures were done by the author and a team of evaluators in association with the Center for the Study of Social Policy and the Annie E. Casey Foundation. Site visits for the analysis presented here were concentrated in Savannah, Georgia, but included Little Rock, Arkansas. Outcome data was collected and evaluated by Metis and Associates. Interview work in the Beacon communities was conducted by the author on site visits in 1995. In both cases interview work was supplemented with documentation reports by funders. See especially, the Center for the Study of Social Policy's *New Futures: Results of a Groundbreaking Social Experiment in Five Cities* (1995) and *A Documentation Report on the New York City Beacons Initiative* (1993). Further information on interviews and analysis can be obtained through the author.

to address these indicators, Foundation advisors argued that social services had to be delivered "more efficiently and effectively." They concluded that this could best be done through a process of collaborating across the institutional boundaries of social service agencies. The Casey Foundation described the intent of New Futures in this way:

> "New Futures" is an attempt . . . to reshape the basic policies and practices of those institutions which help determine the preparation and prospects of young people. . . . The New Futures program seeks to make long-term changes in the operation, principles and policies by which education, employment and other youth services are administered, financed and delivered . . . in government and the private sector. (Annie E. Casey Foundation 1988, 101)

The initiative was designed around a central strategy. Each city would establish an "oversight collaborative" body charged with governance responsibilities. The central tasks of this oversight collaborative were to: (1) identify youth problems; (2) develop strategies and set timelines for addressing these problems; and (3) coordinate multi-institutional responses to these problems. In order to bring these institutions to the table, the Foundation recognized that they needed to offer some incentive for restructuring collaboratively. Casey committed between five and twelve million dollars to each city and required a commitment of local matching funds from public or private agencies. This money was to be used to construct, or rather reconstruct, programs around the goal of cross-institutional collaboration to address the problems of families and youth designated "at risk."

From this bare-bones account of the design of New Futures much can already be said about the logic of the Foundation's approach. For instance, the Casey Foundation's vision of the problem to be addressed focused on ineffectiveness as a product of communication gaps between institutions. Therefore, their vision of the solution was a coordinated, multi-institutional effort at better communication and collaborative decision making, and an effort to eliminate redundancies in services and to share information across the boundaries between institutions currently conceptualized as autonomous. As I will argue later in this chapter, there is an alternative explanation for the ineffectiveness of programs. This explanation focuses on communication gaps as well. However, the problem of communication is not viewed primarily as a lack of communication between directors or supervisors of autonomous agencies, but rather between institutions of service delivery generally and the populations they serve. This alternative understanding locates the roots of ineffectiveness in the lack of voice for "recipients" in the current structure of service delivery.[4] I argue that the communication problem is not chiefly a technical communication problem; it is a political one. Its remedy is not, therefore, merely sharing information in the form in which it currently exists; it is a matter of considering how this information is generated — by whom and about what — raising questions about its interpretation and its uses.

I will explore these questions in the course of this chapter. For now, I simply want to note two things. First, among those designing New Futures programs, the dominant vision of "the problem" was as technical — a matter that required experts to collaborate with other experts, presuming that consensus on more efficient methods of service delivery would be the outcome. Second, the paradigm within which the project was designed and implemented tended to view all problems as *deriving* from a lack of adequate expertise.

Yet when I say that this was the dominant vision of the problem, I do not want to suggest that it was the only one. It was the vision that won out. This is what makes the case of New Futures a particularly interesting one for our purposes. *There was an emphasis in the original design on the importance of including recipients of services in the process of collaboration.* The primary vehicle for this was a system of case management. The Foundation mandated that each city put into place a system of case management to (1) broker services from various agencies on behalf of youth and their families; (2) provide advocates for youth at risk who would also be friends, mentors, and significant adults in their lives; and (3) serve as

4. In the final two chapters, I deal with the relationship between voice and control. I understand that "voice," if it is not connected with real power in the process of decision making, often goes unheard or ignored. Briefly, voice must be understood both as heard and responded to (though not necessarily affirmatively) in order for there to be some relationship between voice and control. It should be noted that the need for greater voice on the part of recipients is recognized in much of the literature in social work. In particular, during the late 1960s and early '70s there were some concerted efforts to incorporate "indigenous nonprofessionals" into the bureaucracy in an attempt to give voice. For analyses of these efforts, see Brager 1965, Loewenberg 1968, Cudaback 1969, and Hardcastle 1971. A key theme in much of this literature is that nonprofessionals tended to be unheeded within the agencies, or alternatively that nonprofessionals were incorporated into the bureaucracy but in the course of integration they lost the connection to the community that had allowed them to serve as its voice. Identification with the community and identification with the bureaucracy seemed to be defined in opposition to one another.

the "eyes and ears of the collaborative" in order to provide information and feedback about policy and practice.

From the perspective of those within the Foundation, this last function was to be particularly important. Case managers were to serve as critical connections between collaborative board members, agency directors, local CEOs — the superintendent, for example — and the community they served. In several cities there was a strong emphasis on case managers being from, living in, or having a history of association with the "community at risk." In one city this was a formal qualification for the job. In addition, the executive director in this city sought people who had no previous connection with service agencies in the area. His aim was to put together a team of people with whom recipients felt comfortable and who would be responsible for communicating with the collaborative about conditions in the community being served. The direct participation of parents and youth was also encouraged, at least formally, in the Foundation's directives to the cities.

In suggesting that case managers were the "eyes and ears" of the collaboratives, the Foundation seemed to recognize the need for information to flow to the collaborative board from the communities designated "at risk." One might have expected that, in light of this, the participation of families and case managers (or "advocates," as they were sometimes called) would have been standard fare in the course of collaborative board meetings. However, despite Foundation mandates for such participation, in none of the five cities did regular participation of this kind occur. Indeed, the participation of, or representation by, case manager/advocates and/or families themselves occurred only a few times anywhere after the first two years. While this may not surprise many observers, in a project of this size, involving fifty million dollars in Foundation money and equal financial commitments by cities, counties, or states, it is very significant that there was not more accountability to this part of the original project design.

First, it suggests that there was little follow-up on the part of the Foundation to enforce such participation. Such a hands-off policy hardly applied in other arenas. The Foundation did not make an across-the-board policy of staying on the sidelines. While Casey gave the cities much leeway in some areas, they dictated many changes, for example, in the *organization* of case management. Yet they failed to enforce the participation of case managers in collaborative decision making. Even after early indicators seemed to suggest that collaboration was not having the desired impact on outcomes, the Foundation did not push participation of case managers or families as a way of redefining the problem or restructuring solutions for the collaborative to address.

Given that such participation was one of the few explicit directives at the outset of the project, two follow-up questions arise: Why didn't case managers and the families for whom they advocated participate in the process of collaborative decision making? And what might have been different if they had?

The Technical Definition of the Problem: Its Impact on Participation

I have suggested that the dominant critique of conventional modes of service delivery focused on the communication and information gaps between separate social service institutions rather than on the gap between these providers and those who were recipients of services. Such a critique frames the problem so that it suggests a technical solution: effective information flow would close the gaps. Those who had relevant information—"experts," directors, supervisors of public and private service agencies, the "right people"—merely needed to sit down and share it. From there, building a consensus on action was taken to follow naturally. The "right people" were explicitly defined in the Foundation directives: city managers, school superintendent, local business, and church and community leadership. The importance of clout was openly acknowledged. Having local leadership of this kind on board at the outset was a key to a city being selected for funding.

This strategy, combined with case management, was supposed to produce an approach that was simultaneously top-down and bottom-up, both "high-level and inclusive." Yet despite this explicit commitment to inclusion, the structure of participation was largely determined by the priority of closing the gaps between institutions. This meant that getting those who headed these institutions on board was key.

At the conclusion of five years of funding, a comprehensive set of evaluative interviews was done with collaborative board members in each of the cities. When the question of bottom-up participation was posed to one former city director, he said of case manager/advocates, "I guess I just never thought they were relevant to the decisions we were making." And when I asked one Foundation evaluator about the neglected commitment to direct participation on the part of recipients, he responded, "Not to sound racist here . . . but do you honestly think you are going to get the city manager to listen to some black welfare mother?!" As disturbing as his comment was, it revealed an important truth: to be politically meaningful, "voice" must be spoken in a context where it is heard. It involves a deeper sense of *collective* responsibility than merely allowing speech. It involves a commitment to listen and, I will argue, ultimately requires a set of institutional arrangements in which decision making is both inclusive and egalitarian.[5]

Several of the interviews we did in the final evaluation of the project assisted us in understanding the resistance on the part of collaborative boards to representation from the "target population." First, to a remarkable extent in two of the five cities, collaborative board members managed to tell themselves and evaluators that New Futures had largely been a success *without* the participation of advocates and families, despite the fact that there was no evidence that the goals each city set at the outset for the population designated "at risk" had been positively affected. Given their understanding of the root of the problem as the need for greater technical expertise and information sharing, several collaborative board members, from representatives of the business community to directors of United Way, were able to point to the existence of the oversight collaborative itself as a success. The willingness of those who headed local systems to work together was a key prerequisite for selecting the cities for Foundation funding. And after five years, at least two of the cities could brag that their efforts at collaboration had successfully brought institutional leaders together. In Savannah one representative of the United Way said that she was extremely encouraged and optimistic about the leadership development she attributed to collaboration. She was particularly impressed with the cooperation of private and public agencies and noted that she was excited about New Futures as a kind of leadership development agency: "What

5. For example, one study concluded that indigenous nonprofessionals incorporated into social work bureaucracies often failed "to facilitate communication between the low-income resident and conventional personas and institutions. Within the agency, nonprofessional staff tend to be unheeded, except in their own particular programs. Their efforts with outside institutions are even more disappointing. As persons of minority group status, without material or educational attainment, they are frequently dismissed by the personnel of the large service systems, barely accorded legitimacy in their official contacts with them. Language difficulty, lack of 'polish,' and working-class status create a gulf. Their advocacy of their people and their cause widen it" (Hardcastle 1971). Within the context of traditional bureaucratic arrangements, voice tends to be co-opted or go unheard.

we've done best will last the longest — it's how we do business. It wasn't just another initiative. It was an environmental change." This "environmental change" was the oversight collaborative itself. Getting the "right people" together in a room once a month was viewed as so critical a part of the remedy that it was often confused with the solution itself, and some members lost sight of a vision of success that actually positively influenced outcomes for families in the "target population." This begins to suggest the insularity of the collaborative as what Fraser has called a kind of "specialized public."

Some collaborative members were more focused on the lack of results in telling the story of collaboration. For them, given the resources, both financial and technical, that had been invested in the project, explaining the lack of positive impact was difficult. Some suggested that five years was too short a time frame in which to expect real results; others looked at U.S. cities as a whole and predicted that without New Futures conditions would have gotten worse.

Perhaps there is some truth in both of these suggestions. But what then would it have taken to make a difference? Surprisingly, in the final evaluation, none of the city directors felt more money would have made a positive difference. And, predictably, some of the directors felt the Foundation had played too intrusive a role, had dictated too many changes too rapidly without adequate information or concern for the particularities of each city. "Foundation people never had a dialogue of give and take with the cities; they determined what kind of technical assistance and who would deliver it," said one director. But even the executive directors did not seem to feel this adequately explained the disparity between initial expectations, expectations that they shared with the Foundation, and outcomes over the five-year period.

So what was the predominant explanation of the inadequacy of New Futures? The study published by Foundation evaluators based on five years of data collection and interview work concludes with a chapter on "lessons learned." The section entitled "Toward the Next Generation of Community-Based Initiatives" offers the following analysis:

> Several of the New Futures cities were successful at creating a political vehicle for change that became a potent force in the community acting on behalf of at-risk youth and their families. But the area of greatest difficulty appeared to be translating cross-agency discourse into *tangible operational reforms* that would improve the status of

youth. *Lack of knowledge about how* to do this — above all else — frustrated the collaboratives' efforts to assist vulnerable children and youth.[6]

And the report continues:

> The New Futures collaboratives had the right view of the prob-lem — namely one that required multiple institutions to solve — but they were generally *unable to come up with strategies* that went beyond discrete categorical interventions. The next generation of community-based collaboratives needs to engage in more ongoing strategic planning. . . . *Key stakeholders* need to be given the time and information to spin out various models, asking whether a par-ticular intervention will work for *a given end.* . . .
>
> The kind of structured operational planning that allows for sys-tematic exploration of various alternatives was pioneered by the RAND Corporation during and shortly after World War II when the United States was faced with critical defense choices. Teams of researchers analyzed alternative scenarios for such things as whether and how to develop U.S. air bases overseas and how to ensure national security in times of international crisis.[7]

One could hardly imagine a tighter fit with Fraser's description of "expert needs discourse." Seven years after its inception, the vision of "the prob-lem" and its solution remain largely unchanged despite the failure of New Futures to reach its stated goals. "Above all else" it was the lack of "knowledge" about *how* to improve outcomes that frustrated collabora-tives. So what is needed? More teams of researchers to do more systematic analysis of alternative scenarios, more planning by key stakeholders. In a meeting with executive directors from the New Futures programs in each city, they too said that the problem was not material resources (they all agreed that they would have been no better able to create systemic change had they had more money), but rather inadequate time to plan. In some cities the planning period had been as abbreviated as six months. There is doubtless some validity to this explanation.

However, what is interesting about this version of "the problem" and its proposed solution is all that remains either unsaid or unchallenged about

6. Center for the Study of Social Policy 1995, 189, emphasis mine.
7. Ibid., 190, emphasis mine.

the process of planning: Who is included? Who is excluded? How does conflict in this process unfold? The "strategic planning" advocated here as necessary to "problem solving" comes out of a particular set of social formations — think tanks like RAND. And again, the term "specialized public" seems to apply. The political implications of such a "specialized public" controlling the planning process is that it is possible to assume consensus, or a higher degree of consensus, on a "given end" because dissenting voices have largely been excluded from the process of planning. Debate within the "specialized public" then focuses on operationalization. Where discussion takes the goal of policy for granted and proceeds as though the issue on the table is "merely an implementation problem," the knowledge that will count for the most is knowledge of how the system as it is currently organized works. This knowledge will most often be the intellectual property of those who wield power as directors, managers, CEOs, and council members in the system as it is currently structured.

We might want to ask the question explicitly: What kind of knowledge do we need to inform our practices of public care? What kind of knowledge is lacking in the conventional approach? The Foundation provided each city with sophisticated models for data collection and the technical assistance to do it. Is more of the same what is needed? From the perspective of many case managers, this data did not constitute knowledge relevant to their strategic planning. One case manager expressed a sentiment shared by most case managers I interviewed: "All I can remember is these people inputting data, and I'm like, 'why are we doing this?' 'Well we need that data-base.' And it's like it didn't get *at* anything." Another case manager commented, "Just looking at the numbers isn't going to give you the whole story. You have to be able to talk about it. That's why I'm so supportive of presenting case studies [to the collaborative]." Moving beyond the numbers to the particularities of each case was in her mind crucial to getting "the whole story."

As "advocates," the case managers in Savannah differentiated themselves from case managers for other agencies because of their belief in the strengths of the community of people with which they worked. "DFACS [Department of Family and Children Services] has a bad reputation. They are always blaming [recipients] for the situation. Sometimes the case managers at DFACS yell at people for being late. But you don't know, maybe that person walked ten miles to get there." And the liaison person for the New Futures church-based day care program commented, "DFACS is known for a kind of us/them mentality [with respect to recipients]." Most of the case managers I interviewed described the problem with traditional services as the adoption of a kind of "us versus them" attitude on the part of providers toward recipients. They repeatedly emphasized the way in which the struggle for better programs must avoid this attitude by recognizing the strengths of the neighborhoods they worked in (and often themselves resided in) and recognizing the importance of the knowledge that comes with living in the community. It was at least in part this understanding of the community as a site of strengths and community members as sources of important knowledge that explains the consistent emphasis among case managers on the need for their participation in reform to be "community rather than agency driven."

Among those who lived in the communities designated "at risk" there was a strong sense that the agenda of the agencies involved in New Futures was not necessarily their agenda. A member of one black organization, Guardians of the Culture, suggested:

> The black community knows that our agenda is not their agenda. There is strength in knowing that. There is strength in knowing that so we can organize to support our agenda. . . . Guardians of the Culture is not included in their vision. There are a lot of people not included. . . . Annie E. Casey doesn't need to keep giving the same old people money. You put your faith into the community.

"Faith in the community," in this view, seems to be linked to a belief in the strengths of the community. She commented on the misplaced pathologizing of the community — "One 'bad house' on the block and suddenly everyone else is thinking the whole neighborhood has problems" — and she stressed the importance of living in the community for knowing the community.

Similarly, one community member objected strongly to a debate that was going on regarding the establishment of an Afro-centric school for boys. The problem with the debate, as she saw it, was the identity of the participants. The head of the local NAACP was opposed to the school; the executive director of New Futures supported it, as did she. But that, she said, was not the point:

> He [the Executive Director of Savannah New Futures] should have had the mothers, rather than taking on the NAACP himself. We should have been the task force. [He] could have packed the room

with mothers. If I had been involved I would have packed the room with women. They would have had signs, and the NAACP would have said, "Well let's sit down and talk about this . . ." What were they thinking!!! . . . We gave birth to these boys. And another thing about that task force — who lives with these boys? Who takes care of them? It's the women.

Among case manager/advocates and community members as well, there was a consistent emphasis on the need to recognize that community members, "the target population," had the strength and the knowledge to represent themselves in the course of defining needs.

However, the kinds of knowledge that advocates thought of as necessary to the collaborative process tended to be quite different in form and content than those used by collaborative board members. These rival conceptions of what knowledge counted had critical implications for participation. The description of strategic planning offered earlier leaves unstated who the participants in this process are, with the exception of several references like "key stakeholders" and "community leaders." A quote from the *Strategic Planning Guide* put together at the outset of the Foundation effort is illustrative here:

> Real involvement has to come from senior decision-makers: the mayor, union leaders, CEO's, the school superintendent, private agency directors, state policy officials, school board members, juvenile court judges, officers of the PTA, and the leaders of grass-roots community organizations. Without this level of representation community planning will not have the prestige to create a visible community priority on youth, nor will it have the political authority to convert that priority into meaningful institutional reform. (Annie E. Casey Foundation 1988, 103)

"Political authority" and "prestige" are the justifications for participation, so it is perhaps not all that surprising that in no city did substantial participation from grass-roots organizations occur. As one collaborative board member noted, "One concern I had early on was the fact that the minority-run, the African-American and the Latino organizations, were not part of the process at all. Not because we didn't want them to be part of the process. We actively went out and sought their support. They just were not there at all." While "buy-in" on the part of these groups may have been sought, their active and critical participation in the process of defining needs and an agenda for meeting them was not. In light of this, their support was difficult to achieve. They were "not there" for Foundation efforts. Again, this is despite explicit commitments to the contrary on the part of the Foundation. For example, again from the *Strategic Planning Guide:*

> Inclusive community participation is not being recommended for its own sake. Instead, it is a practical necessity. Very simply, people and agencies who are not involved in helping to define a problem are unlikely to be involved effectively in solving it. (Annie E. Casey Foundation 1988, 102)

While there is a consistent emphasis, at least in the original Foundation directives, on the need for collaborative participation that is both high level and inclusive, the concern is largely for participation as a process of *buying into* an already existing vision of the solution, a "given end," and constructing a forum for working out implementation problems.

Oversight collaborative members clearly bought into this vision. Speaking about representatives on the collaborative board, one member commented,

> They cannot be just anybody. You have to have someone, representatives of those institutions, it seems to me, that when they speak somebody listens. . . . So while those institutions, I totally agree, have to be there, I think you also have to get enough diversity and enough — I hate to use the word *power* because it's one I don't like to use — but enough people to come to the table, that can influence how decisions are made in that collective.

He went on to suggest as examples of diversity a county judge or the superintendent. Another member of the collaborative board reflected on the five-year process of collaborative building and described it in the following terms:

> We deliberately set out to try and form a Board with clout, a top-down one that could and would be looked to because of the resources and institutional strength that was there . . . to try to renaissance a variety of things. . . . It's too soon to know whether this one

will work, but we have major corporate people. We have the head
of the County Commissioners, the Mayor, the City Council, United
Way, the Universities, the Foundations, small businesses and community representatives. These people have been selected through a
very careful process of trying to figure out what they would present
both in terms of broad presence on the Board and what they represent in terms of power — the ability to communicate and to deliver
on matters, common causes and concerns.

These descriptions reflect the common assumption that those who have the
political authority and prestige to make themselves heard with other members of the collaborative board have authority with the population generally. But as interviews with members of the "target" population revealed,
political authority of this kind almost immediately translated into a lack of
legitimacy in the community designated "at risk." The sense that "their
agenda is not our agenda" was strong. A deep sense of distrust followed
from this. Some collaborative personnel recognized this and sought to hire
case managers who did not have a history of affiliation with traditional
service bureaucracies and were preferably residents in the target communities. But the problem of trust remained. As one case manager argued,
"The agencies don't seem to understand reform as turning power over to
others." The concern to have on board those with the prestige to be lis-
tened to, as one community member put it, quickly led to the vision of
New Futures as "just one more bureaucracy."

Neutrality and Consensus in the Planning Process

Embedded in the language of high-level and inclusive participation was the
assumption that bringing the "right people" together would produce a
consensus. The instructions that cities received for the construction of the
oversight collaborative are illustrative:

One option may be the creation of a formal "planning/oversight
collaborative" — that is a new organization governed by a board of
participating sector representatives, whose purpose is to carry out

the community-wide planning and oversight functions involved in the New Futures initiative. . . .

Another option could be the designation of an existing organization in the community that has a reputation or capacity to serve as a *neutral convener* for an inclusive planning process. (Annie E. Casey Foundation 1988, 104)

The Foundation's early vision of the project reflected an astonishing faith that "collaboration" among the right people — "participating sector representatives" — would produce consensus. Everyone could agree that the conditions faced by youth were unacceptable. From there the question seemed merely one of agreeing on how these problems should be addressed. But a technical definition of the problem, a focus on operationalization, did not, in practice, actually translate into a consensus among experts. There were, for example, heated political debates about how exactly redundant services should be eliminated: Which agency was to relinquish control? What did this mean for budget concerns in the future? How was accountability going to be restructured to accommodate collaborative arrangements? All of these questions were clearly political — that is, they were about who should control resources and why — rather than matters resolvable by reference to some accepted body of expert advice. To some extent, it is remarkable that the Foundation did not anticipate these dilemmas, but rather assumed that a broad consensus on the need to help youth and families designated "at risk" would facilitate a deeper consensus on how this should be done. It did not.

As one city manager noted in the five-year evaluation, in practice there was much disagreement about the sources of the problem; and upon further discussion, this often pointed to a disagreement about the nature of the problem itself: "We need to begin with a community consensus that *this* is a problem. . . . I'm not sure there is a community consensus that *this* is a problem." For example, while there may have been broad agreement among collaborative board members that teen pregnancy was undesirable, whether "the problem" was too much sex education in the schools, as one collaborative member contended, or too little as others contended, was a matter of much dispute. And perhaps more important, many teens in "inner-city" Savannah did not seem to share in the consensus that teen pregnancy was the problem. Frontline staff we spoke with, all of whom supported sex education in the schools, also noted that many girls came to them to find out how to get pregnant, when during the month they were most likely to conceive. And they noted that many of these teens had limited opportunities for further education and career development; unemployment in some New Futures communities was 30 percent and higher, and access to continuing education was limited by inadequate information and financial resources. To many teens, pregnancy seemed a rational choice. In a situation such as this, a sex education curriculum that attempts to discourage pregnancy by focusing on lost opportunities for advanced education and career may be missing the point.

Furthermore, while there may have been a fairly broad consensus that high rates of unemployment were not a good thing, there were very different understandings of why this should be viewed as a problem. For instance, one executive director spoke about how he had lured the business community into collaborative involvement with the line "We pay now or we pay later" — either we invest dollars in job training now or we support these kids on welfare with our tax dollars later. But framing the need for care in these terms was problematic. From the perspective of business, "the problem" became fairly exclusively that of producing a trained labor force that they could separate from the issue of a decently paid labor force. And even if it produced a consensus on the need to help youth "at risk," the consensus was a rather artificial one. "Well trained" often meant something different to the business community and the Department of Labor than "well educated" meant to educators. Yet schools were the institutions primarily responsible for ensuring job readiness.

The point here is that the Foundation often assumed that taking an institutionally integrated approach to their agenda for "at risk" families meant that inclusion would translate easily into consensus. Where there was a consensus among collaborative board members that a particular social trend was a problem, teen pregnancy for example, they frequently disagreed about the sources and therefore about the remedies for addressing the problem. Perhaps most important, a consensus among collaborative board members did not mean it was shared among members of the "target population." And while frontline workers, school nurses, case managers, parents, and teens recognized that addressing teen pregnancy and meeting the needs of teen mothers was far more complicated than a new sex education curriculum, they had no voice in collaborative decision making, so this information was never introduced to debate strategies for dealing with teen pregnancy.

Neutrality, Consensus, and Participation:
The View from the "Bottom" Up

In one city, collaborative board members noted the advantages of the size of the city to the process of collaboration. A representative of the Chamber of Commerce commented, "We used to joke that it was the same 200 people in Savannah who did everything." And a representative of United Way commented that the size of Savannah had facilitated the success of New Futures: "We trip over each other all the time. We see each other all the time, at meetings, in organizations." Savannah is a city of 150,000. It is unlikely that "we" here refers to all 150,000, so the question is again relevant: Who is included and who is excluded from that "same 200"? What difference might it have made if the participants had been advocates or recipients themselves?

The reference to the "same 200" was suggested both by those in the circle of the "same 200 who do everything" and those outside of it. But many who understood themselves as outsiders would hardly have attributed the success of New Futures to the direction of this select group. Rather, they looked to it to explain its failures: "Their agenda is not our agenda." And as one more sympathetic community member commented, "It's not that they don't want to help us, it's that *they* don't know how."

Despite a strategy that was supposedly simultaneously top-down and bottom-up, there was not much question in anybody's mind about which strategy had prevailed. Of Savannah, one collaborative member commented self-consciously that though he thought they were getting more grass-roots-oriented, "There is no way that someone on the Authority [New Futures] could go into the neighborhood [the target area] and become part of it."

Again, there were people who headed programs for New Futures who recognized that this was a problem. The site manager for the Family Resource Center in Savannah had only recently come on board with New Futures. She noted that she hoped to avoid many of the mistakes she felt other programs had made by failing to include the community residents in governing. She commented that there was a need to recognize the "expertise that comes with the experience of living." As a resident of the community she served, she noted that there was a marked lack of trust on the part of her fellow residents toward any social service program: "They [social programs] keep getting people to the middle of the bridge, but then there is no continuation . . . there is no community involvement," she explained. Savannah, and in particular her community within Savannah, had been a pilot site for efforts by several foundations, and disillusionment with such programs on the part of the residents was fairly pervasive.

Further, and importantly, she argued that the reason for the lack of community involvement was that those who designed programs had often pathologized the community to such an extent that they did not think such participation was appropriate. This was particularly true in Savannah, where the boundaries of the "community at risk" were established by literally mapping the pathologies. Residency in "Area C" defined the "target population." It was the area with the highest rate of residential burglaries, homicides, public disorder complaints, aggravated assaults, "incidents involving juveniles," child abuse and neglect, dilapidated housing, and teen pregnancy.[8] Understood in these terms, it is no wonder that the neighborhoods that constituted Area C were not seen as strengths upon which to build but rather as problems that needed to be solved. The site manager, however, offered an alternative perspective on her neighborhood: "There is maybe one 'bad house' on the block, but they ignore the rest and focus on that one."

This was a consistent theme in discussions with case managers as well. But it was a theme that went largely ignored by the collaborative boards. In Bridgeport, for example, case managers spoke of attempts to communicate with the collaborative board and claimed, "They treated us as though we didn't know what we were talking about." And, "As a representative of the Hispanic community I felt they [the collaborative board] did not speak my language, they simply could not understand." The barrier was not simply Spanish versus English. The case manager was perfectly fluent in both languages. Rather she was referring to an unwillingness on the part of the board to engage the information the case managers were presenting. One of her colleagues in case management commented, "It is like they [the

8. For more on the social construction of communities that are the site of study, see Schneider and Ingram (1993, 334), who argue that the construction of target populations is an important, "albeit overlooked political phenomenon." By social construction of target populations they mean "the cultural characterizations of popular images of the person or groups whose behavior and well-being is affected by public policy." Citing the work of Murray Edelman, they note that these characterizations are normative and evaluative, portraying groups in positive or negative terms. Thus, while the Foundation treated the portrayal of Area C as merely a collection of facts, it is possible to imagine mapping the strengths rather than the pathologies of communities.

collaborative] are in a different world, [like] there are two different worlds, speaking different languages." A case manager in Savannah suggested that what was needed for effective communication was "honesty— there has to be the honesty to say, 'I don't know what goes on in your world, why don't you tell me?'"

Nor did the view from the bottom up tend to support the vision of neutrality offered in the Foundation directives. Case managers as well as several of the community members with whom I spoke did not see the Foundation's issuing invitations to all the "key stakeholders" as a "neutral" position. As noted earlier, for many this was interpreted as "Casey being just another bureaucracy," where *bureaucracy* was a term that evoked images, not of neutrality, but of "us versus them."

An Alternative Vision of Community Collaboration

It is not my objective here to fully elaborate an alternative vision of community collaboration. Rather, I have suggested in the first three sections of this chapter what the politics of care in the context of a conventional institutional arrangement look like. Those who are treated in this system of care as "dependent" are seen as lacking the capacity to participate in defining their own needs. Even where there may be a recognition, as in the case of New Futures' original design, that "buy-in" on the part of recipients was important, the knowledge necessary to defining and meeting needs was located in an institutionalized class of caregivers—here represented by the collaborative board. It is the relatively fixed positioning of this class of caregivers in relation to a class of "cared-fors" that makes paternalistic practices—experts speaking for clients or cases in the process of defining needs—difficult to avoid. The absence of voice on the part of the "needy" tends to mean that resources, both human and material, invested for the purpose of care, often fail to meet needs.

In what follows, I will describe an alternative institutional arrangement that suggests the potential of public care modeled on more mutual rather than paternalistic relationships. Then I will suggest how community members viewed the practices of care as they unfolded in this institutional context.

The Beacons programs, like those of New Futures, are school-community collaboration projects. They are located in schools throughout the

New York City metropolitan area. In response to community concerns that in many neighborhoods, kids had literally no place to go after school hours, the mayor allocated ten million dollars of the City's "Safe Streets, Safe Cities" fund to establish school-based community centers. The Beacons projects began in 1991 with a commitment to keep school buildings open for extended hours. Now some Beacons programs advertise that they are open 360 days a year.

After only two years in operation, Beacons typically enrolled approximately 1,000 community residents as ongoing participants. The highest annual enrollment was 1,848; the lowest, 628. Average daily attendance at the twenty Beacons programs was 203. Typically Beacons served 40–60 adults per week in adult education classes, including computer literacy, conversational English, and entrepreneurship courses. They provide youth and adults with a mix of social services and recreational, educational, and vocational services. Through Beacons, young people have an opportunity to participate in activities ranging from drama to sports, leadership development and entrepreneurial programs, peer education and counseling, and community service. At most Beacons, members are asked to volunteer in a range of roles, such as assisting with security, tutoring children, planning and facilitating, family nights, and participating in neighborhood projects. They were viewed as successful enough that by July 1992, the city committed to doubling the number of Beacons from the original ten to twenty communities (Cahill et al. 1993, 11).

What is different about the Beacons projects is that when the city of New York committed itself to these projects, they sought out community organizations geographically located in the neighborhoods surrounding Beacons schools to run the programs. They assumed that success was dependent on a sense of ownership by the neighborhood, the "target population," and that this sense of ownership was most likely if an organization with established history and credibility in the neighborhoods was given the authority to manage the resource base for the Beacons. Understanding that "authority with whom?" was a relevant question to be asked, the Beacons program adopted a very different strategic plan than had New Futures. They handed over resources, with minimal accountability, to these community-based organizations. These organizations then turned to their members, residents of the community, to design and implement programs. Increasing the "opportunities for caring relationships" among residents was the primary goal of the Beacons programs (Cahill et al. 1993, 6).

What impact did this have on the practices of care in the Beacons program? First, it almost immediately broke down any permanent distinction between caregivers and those cared for. At one Beacon program, all of the street outreach coordinators who designed and organized programs are members of the community-based organization, use its facilities and programs, and have lived in the community and have families who use the Beacons programs. As outreach coordinators, they participate with a community board in a process of decision making about which services the local Beacons program should offer and which are going to be subcontracted out. In all the Beacons this was a carefully made decision. For unlike New Futures, Beacons planners had a very strong sense that the work of "care" ought to be done as much as possible *by* community members for other community members. The director of one Beacons program commented, "Everything filters down. If the design assumes pathology, that filters down. If you hire outsiders, you're not sending the message that the help is here in the community." She noted that the "sick community thesis" was embedded in the guidelines for funding for many public and privately sponsored projects and that there was a strong commitment to avoiding this in the Beacons program. This was facilitated by rejecting a division of labor in which governance of services was done by one class of providers for a separate class of recipients. Community members were seen as resources, and the Beacons as a site to facilitate the sharing of resources. In creating a kind of network for mutual caretaking, there was again an explicit rejection of traditional models of service delivery:

> Well, you can't really have anyone else come into your neighborhood, you know, look through your neighborhood for maybe a week or a month and say, "OK, these are the problems we've seen. OK, this is what this neighborhood needs," without asking for the community's input and things like that. Other organizations I've seen—they have this whole elitist attitude. Like, "we've gone through this training, we have this knowledge. We're coming into this community: You don't know anything you're doing, that's why your community is like this, so we're just going to like do everything for you. You're just going to sit back and we're going to take all the glory." But what is different about the Beacons is that no decisions really are made within the Beacons without the community's involvement.

"Community" here is not established through the process of a city manager's office constructing a "target population" by mapping rates of homicide, child neglect, and teen pregnancy. Rather, the program is put into place in a geographical location in which residents already understand themselves as part of a shared community.[9] The description offered of this shared community is revealing. In each Beacons program I visited, neighborhoods that were characterized by nonresidents as "bad" or "dangerous" were described quite differently by residents on the Beacons staff. One Beacons staffer, a young black man, commented:

> I would describe it as a really colorful community. There is a list of different types of people that live here: there is the working class, there are people who are struggling with school and with children, there are people who go to church daily, there are people who hang out on corners and just play cards or dominoes, stuff like that. Besides that, there is a list of problems within the community not unlike any other community. You have the drug problem, a crime problem, you have your rifts with this black and that black, you have your teen pregnancy and your racial problems.

Such a vision of the community is a significant reason why staffers felt comfortable both identifying themselves as members and residents, and promoting broad-based participation of community members in the process of program decision making. While they recognized conflicts within their community, they saw it as essentially "not unlike any other community," and certainly did not see it as essentially a community of dependents. This strong identity with the community was a feature of the staff in all of the Beacons I visited, as was the emphasis on the community as a site of strengths rather than an exclusive focus on pathologies.

One staffer related the importance of community identity directly to the problem of determining needs:

> I think it's crucial that the community does its own needs assessment. You can't have someone come in from bougie [bourgeoisie] town up there and say, "Well, listen, I heard — read the papers — I heard you are having this kind of problem. I think this is the solu-

9. This was facilitated by the existence of the community-based organizations, many of which had long histories in the neighborhoods, as well as by the fact that most of these programs were located in schools that were neighborhood schools. Furthermore, this sense of community was often facilitated by a shared racial or ethnic identity, as in the case of the program run by Alianza, which is located in a neighborhood with a very large Dominican population.

tion. This is great, look at my program. . . ." I think the community really needs to say, "Well, listen, I know that this guy is on the corner every day, and I know that my children can't pass through there."

The staffers recognized that this process of needs assessment was fundamentally different from the process that occurs in more traditional service delivery.[10] But they stressed that this approach to needs assessment was necessary to avoiding the elitism of conventional approaches (an elitism that they noted produced trust and communication problems), to recognizing strengths in the community (by hiring community residents to do needs assessment), and to getting needs "right" in some sense. Staffers were constantly contrasting their own dispositions with those of traditional service providers; they positioned themselves, not as professionals who know what is good for recipients, but rather as facilitators. This was clear in their description of needs assessment:

> You've got to get the person comfortable to know that you're not going to go, "I'm here, I'm an outreach coordinator, Youth Department Services. What do you need?" No, you go out, get acquainted. And you tap into what this person is feeling or where this person is at, what does this person want to do. . . . I'm not being told, "Well, find out how many of these youth need jobs." I'm not being told, "Go with a piece of paper and get me as many names as you can of people who need jobs." I'm going out there asking "What do you need?" And they are telling me, "We need jobs."

This coordinator recognizes that *how* information is gathered, *how* needs are assessed, matters. Even where the information gathered might be similar to findings in more traditional modes of needs assessment, the descrip-

10. Brager (1965) made similar observations. In his study of nonprofessional staff who had been incorporated into social work bureaucracies, he observes, "The nonprofessional tends to give stronger weight to external life circumstances than to internal factors. In instances when caseworkers have defined clients as 'neglectful,' nonprofessional staff have been more likely to see the behavior as a response to depressed conditions" (37). He relates competing interpretations of need directly to these varying assessments of the situation of clients, arguing that the "professional role" of the caseworker often inhibits communication and that nonprofessionals are unencumbered by this. He observes that group loyalty between the nonprofessional and the program participant are evident. Hardcastle (1971) argues that this loyalty is critical to the "special skill" indigenous nonprofessionals have in being attuned to clients' needs.

tion above suggests the importance of not going to the community presuming knowledge of what they need, but rather inviting them to participate in defining their needs.

In rejecting the idea that their communities should be defined in terms of pathologies, Beacons staff were able to locate strengths in the communities, to build programs in which participants shared their resources and their skills. Teens in the neighborhood frequently ran programs for younger children; adults networked organizing workshops — from résumé writing to plant care to parenting tips. The Beacons rejected a model of care that assumed a fixed class of providers in favor of a model of mutual caretaking.

Voice, Participation, and Governance in the Practice of Care

While both New Futures and the Beacons programs represent innovative attempts to reorganize social services, these efforts at school-community collaboration were motivated by very different understandings of the central problem that reform ought to address. New Futures saw the problem as rooted in a lack of communication among providers of social services. By contrast, the Beacons programs recognized a communication problem between providers and recipients. Moreover, they rejected the idea that this could be resolved through buy-in on the part of recipients. More than an invitation to inclusion was required. Beacons staffers recognized that locating the authority to define needs in a fixed class of providers corresponded with the construction of a dependency that is incompatible with participation as equals in the collaborative endeavor. This was a prerequisite to both understanding needs in the community and effectively meeting them. Participation as equals required the reconstruction of relationships of public care.

New Futures had its successes in facilitating better communication between those who control resources. But it seems clear that New Futures, despite its innovations, conformed to conventional assumptions about care that assumed a fixed class of providers and a class of dependents. Providers were further recognized as having the authority to define needs. By contrast, the Beacons programs challenged the assumption that the positions of provider and recipient were fixed. Staffers argued that their community was composed of members who were both providers and recipients of care, often simultaneously. In light of this, the authority to define needs was also challenged. It was viewed as critical that "the community do its own needs assessment." In this final section of this chapter, I offer a comparison of New Futures and the Beacons in an attempt to illustrate the problem of paternalism.

Inclusion of those understood as "recipients" was a theme in both programs. But as I have noted already, the design of New Futures tended to assume that the *inclusion* of multiple institutions of public care *would produce a consensus* among those institutions on policies and policy implementation for youth and families designated "at risk." I do not want to make the same mistake when I advocate the participation of those currently positioned as recipients of care in a network of care. Conflict about how needs are defined, as well as which needs have priority and how they should be met, is inevitable. Locating the practices of care in a network of relationships among relative equals, as in the case of the Beacons, does, however, have advantages when conflicts arise. Where the authority of "providers" in relation to recipients is taken as given, conflict between provider and recipients tends to go unrecognized or to result in the silencing of a class of "dependents." By contrast, in the context of more mutual relationships of care, conflict does not have a formulaic outcome; contestation is open and has the potential to be organized democratically.

The focus of efforts at inclusion differed quite dramatically in the two programs. The New Futures project illustrates well how "expert needs discourse," which evolves out of the institutionalization of a class of caregivers and a class of dependents, rapidly silences those understood as "needy." New Futures makes this particularly clear, for recipients were excluded despite explicit commitments to their inclusion. Given such explicit commitments, why wasn't the inclusion of advocates taken seriously? I have suggested that, given the dominant understanding of "the problem" that collaboration was attempting to address, and given the dominant understanding of what counted as the knowledge necessary to address this problem, inclusion was not necessary to reformulating or reorganizing the practices of care. Inclusion came to be seen as a process of buy-in, and ultimately the emphasis was on those with resources or prestige buying in. After all, those receiving care weren't going to be obstacles to collaboration between service agencies; whatever new policies and practices of care evolved out of collaboration, recipients would still be recipients, subject to the authority of providers.

The terms of inclusion are significant to explaining this. Whether the "target" population is included as "clients or cases" or as "members or participants" strongly affects how participation unfolds — whose voices are heard and who responds to those voices. When case managers were made the "eyes and ears" of the collaborative, the intention, it would seem, should have been to give them "voice." Yet even if case managers had regularly been given the opportunity to serve as "eyes and ears," to tell their story, they might have provided helpful information for policy design. But this would have left unchallenged the division of labor in which a class of providers governs or controls the practices of care. Moreover, to say that "they" make decisions more effectively with better information about the population for which they provide is to say nothing of how well they meet the needs of this population. For in addition to controlling the provision of services, providers define "needs" and "effectiveness" as well. In such a situation, the authority of providers is difficult to challenge, for their "care" is appropriately responsive to "needs" as they understand them. Thus in Savannah the need to collaborate was recognized and successfully addressed as evidenced by the existence of the oversight collaborative board. By the end of five years, the needs of the target population, the impetus for collaboration, had seemingly become a secondary indicator of success. As one board member put it, "What we have done best will last longest — it's how we do business." The business of collaboration was conducted by the same people, and it was still committed to a vision of care that assumed a fixed class of providers and a class understood as "dependent."

Viewed through the lens of Fraser's politics of needs interpretation, we might suggest that this "specialized public" with its "expert needs discourse" was critical to institutionalizing the authority of providers. In Chapter 1, I identified such authority relationships in the context of care as paternalism. Rather than seeing paternalism as intervention in a process of self-regarding decision making — a critique that might imply as the solution the abandonment of programs such as these — I suggest that we reconceptualize the paternalism critique in light of the actual practices of care. The analysis in this chapter suggests that paternalistic authority is exercised *in the process of speaking for others in the course of defining needs*. Such authority is commonly justified with reference to the status of recipients as dependents. Such "dependency" rules out meaningful participation in the process of defining "needs" and "effectiveness," or designing and implementing systems of mutual caretaking.

When I define paternalism as the process of speaking for others in the course of defining needs, I do not want to suggest, however, that voice alone is what matters; it is a necessary, but not sufficient, condition for control. After all, the original design of New Futures was an attempt to give recipients "voice" by making case managers the "eyes and ears" of the collaborative. This language is telling; it makes explicit who has the authority to "give voice" and who, in turn, will control policy after voice is granted. Empowerment in the context of dependency — dependence on outsiders for the provision of services or dependence on them for the recognition of voice — is difficult either to conceptualize or to actualize; for dependence and paternalism are two sides of the same coin.

Framing paternalism in this way suggests why many of those "at risk" rejected New Futures' collaborative model of reform; they began by rejecting the notion that those who received services were *uniquely* or *deviantly* dependent. Rather they saw Area C as a community not that different from any other. They were able to see the strengths of families and neighborhoods and even to view community members as experts of sorts.

Challenging the conventional understanding of what and who counts as having expertise has fairly direct political consequences in this context. The practices of care generally and, more specifically, the practices of defining needs must be understood within the context of a liberal bureaucratic state that plays expertise off against inclusive participation. Such an either/or approach may be unhelpful. One can certainly imagine that, for example, knowing something about the process of city budgeting or having access to a comparative analysis of after-school programs could be of some use in designing and implementing collaborative projects. But expert knowledge of the policy process does not constitute all of the knowledge relevant to understanding needs; "the expertise that comes from living here" is also critical to getting "the whole story," to putting to appropriate use knowledge of the budgetary process or comparable program studies. The authority of traditional experts to define needs is justified by reference to knowledge; by expanding what kind of knowledge counts as relevant, we have expanded who counts as legitimate participants in the process of defining need. We have suggested the importance of both including and responding to voices in the community.

Both frontline workers for New Futures and Beacons staff argued that "the expertise that comes with the experience of living" is crucial to appropriately defining and addressing needs. Many of them, as residents themselves, were "experts" in this sense — experts by virtue of their own practical knowledge about living in the community. In the case of New

Futures, where the practices of care were concerned, frontline workers were viewed as providers but not as policy makers. Policy makers, the recognized experts, "lived in a different world." They were clearly outsiders. By contrast, the Beacons looked to the community as providers and as policy makers as well as people in need.

In addition to recognizing the authority of community participants in defining needs, the Beacons recognized them as a resource for providing care. This required a wholesale rejection of the dependency model that underwrites paternalistic care. As opposed to beginning with a model of the "sick community" in need of experts to heal it, the Beacons programs were premised on the assumption that all members of a community are both providers and recipients of care, often simultaneously. Recognizing the fluidity of these roles was critical to identifying and fostering relationships of mutual care as an alternative to paternalistic care.

3

The Ethic of Care
and the Politics of Need

The previous chapter demonstrated that the practices of public social provision as they are currently organized often evolve paternalistically. I suggested in the first chapter that such criticism, given our liberal orientation in the public sphere, tends to imply abandonment as its alternative rather than more egalitarian relationships of care. What would the framework, both conceptual and institutional, for such mutual caretaking look like? How exactly do the practices of care and justice need to come together to make these relationships possible? The case study of the Beacons programs begins to suggest some possible answers to these questions. Does the conceptual work on care assist us in developing a broader framework for care?

We turn now to Carol Gilligan's foundational work on the ethic of care. This chapter is intended as a brief introduction to this work as well as an exploration of the relationship between the ethic of care and theory that is considered more explicitly political. I offer here a summary that highlights aspects of the "care" literature particularly relevant to this project rather than a thoroughgoing analysis.

As an alternative to traditional approaches to moral decision making, work focused on care is appropriate to this project for two critical reasons. First, work within the care tradition has focused on needs and thus may provide a model for the needs-oriented work of public care. Second, much of this work takes a critical perspective on the conventional forms of moral reasoning by suggesting its inadequacies in practice. The emphasis on practice problematizes notions of a fixed boundary between the moral and the political. We will explore this in greater detail in the following chapter. In light of this emphasis on the actual and the practical, we might then ask, Is the ethic of care as a guide to the practices of public care able to avoid the problem of paternalism? Would it produce a more appropriate understanding of needs? Does an orientation to care address the concern to avoid both domination and neglect? A discussion of work on care provides a forum for raising questions about how in practice the politics of care might differ from the politics of justice. We will begin with a brief overview of the theory of justice that is challenged in work on care.

Justice

Most work on care focuses on developing a critique, if not an outright rejection, of Rawlsian justice. His is certainly not the only theory of justice, but his work and the Kantian project he continues are the focus of attention in the justice/care debates. So it is with his work that we begin.[1]

Rawls understands the principles of justice as principles that "free and rational persons concerned to further their own interests would accept in an initial position of equality as defining the fundamental terms of their association" (11). He calls this "justice as fairness." The principles of justice are arrived at from behind a veil of ignorance "where parties do not know their conceptions of the good or their special psychological propensities" (12). The purpose of the veil of ignorance, according to Rawls, is

1. In-text page citations are to Rawls, *A Theory of Justice* (1971).

to rule out those principles that it would be rational to propose for acceptance, however little the chance of success, only if one knew certain things that are irrelevant from the standpoint of justice. For example, if a man knew that he was wealthy, he might find it rational to advance the principle that various taxes for welfare measures be counted unjust; if he knew that he was poor, he would most likely propose the contrary principle. (18–19)

The self behind the veil of ignorance knows nothing about his particular location or identity in society (140). In fact, Rawls goes so far as to say that those behind the veil of ignorance do not even know the particular circumstances of their own society; they know nothing about its political or economic systems when they think about justice, and this is important to ensuring that the same principles of justice are always chosen. "If a knowledge of particulars is allowed, then the outcome is biased by arbitrary contingencies." He goes on:

If the original position is to yield agreements that are just, the parties must be fairly situated and treated equally as moral persons. The arbitrariness of the world must be corrected for by adjusting the circumstances of the initial contractual situation. Moreover, if in choosing principles we required unanimity even when there is full information, only a few rather obvious cases could be decided. A conception of justice based on unanimity in these circumstances would indeed be weak and trivial. But once knowledge is excluded the requirement of unanimity is not out of place and the fact that it can be satisfied is of great importance. It enables us to say of the preferred conception of justice that it represents a genuine reconciliation of interests. (142)

This reconciliation of interests is made possible by Rawls's vision of the self. What kind of selves are we then, when we are behind the veil of ignorance? We are morally autonomous selves, selves that are described as mutually disinterested and yet not egoistic (128–29). It is not immediately clear how to understand an individual as simultaneously not interested in others and not necessarily egoistic. For if we rule out interest in others, what is left but self-interest and by default selfishness? Rawls here argues that we are mutually disinterested in *actual* others. He goes on to say, however, that such selves still have an interest, for instance, in the idea of an everlasting moral agent, and so they do pursue intergenerational justice again, not out of a particular attachment to one's own children, but out of an attachment to an abstract, everlasting moral agent. This is what makes the interest in future generations consistent with justice.

On this model of justice, admitting particular knowledge threatens the impartiality that makes unanimous agreement on the same principles of justice possible. The strong belief in autonomy makes it possible to argue that our particular attachments to others are contingent relationships with the self rather than constitutive of the self. It also results in a view that people are entitled to noninterference, and in this sense the justice tradition is individualistic. The process of moral reasoning in which a morally autonomous self engages uses reason to discern which principles ought to be followed. On Rawls's model, this reason produces two principles of justice: the first requires equality in the assignment of basic rights and duties. The second holds that social and economic inequalities, for example inequalities of wealth and authority, are just only if they result in compensating benefits for everyone, and in particular for the least advantaged members of society. Note then that from an original position of mutual disinterest, Rawls can still, given the conditions behind the veil of ignorance, produce an argument for institutions that better the plight of the least well off. Such a principle is the inevitable result of an agreement among rational persons concerned to advance their interests but lacking knowledge about their own position within a system of which inequality is one feature. It is relevant to note here that while Rawls is most often invoked as the representative of the justice tradition in the literature on care, he does not emphasize autonomy as economic self-sufficiency in the way that Locke does. Recall that in Locke's original position, the state of nature, there is no problem of scarcity; whereas Rawls says quite clearly that his original position assumes both mutual disinterest and scarcity. This results in different political consequences for their alternative visions of justice. For Locke sees economic inequality as compatible with individual freedoms because there is always, even in cases of dramatic inequalities in wealth, the option for individuals to at least subsist: "Nor was this *appropriation* of any parcel of *Land,* by improving it, any prejudice to any other Man for there was still enough and as good left and more than the yet unprovided could use"(Locke [1690] 1994, 291). For Rawls, by contrast, because scarcity is acknowledged in the original position, in the case of dramatic inequalities it is reasonable to worry; and a free and autonomous person behind the veil of ignorance would worry that such inequalities might leave the least well off very badly off. Hence the commitment to the difference principle. Put simply, Rawls ends up defending something that looks more like a social democracy, while Locke produces the original defense of liberal democracy. Both are theories of justice, but they result in very different political and economic arrangements.

What then do these theories of justice share in common? Eva Kittay and Diana Meyers argue that it is natural rights arguments that define the justice tradition:

> Because people are capable of moral autonomy, they are morally entitled and ought to be legally entitled to conduct their lives as they see fit. Their rights protect them from other's aggression and free them to do what they want, provided that they do not violate others' rights. Locke's list of natural rights — the rights to life, liberty and property — was seminal. Though variously interpreted and supplemented in subsequent theories, this set of rights captures a constant of the justice tradition. People are surely entitled to noninterference; they may not be entitled to aid. Though it is morally commendable to help the needy, and though justice may require helping the needy, it is disputable whether anyone has a *right* to such positive benefits as medical care, decent housing or education. In this respect, the justice tradition is individualistic. The rights it recognizes morally equip people to take care of themselves while morally shielding them both from the demands of others and from the invasiveness of the state. (Kittay and Meyers 1987, 5)

Kittay and Meyers suggest here how claims about moral autonomy easily, if not necessarily, slip into claims about personal autonomy and self-sufficiency. "Shielded from the demands of others" because of moral autonomy, our freedom here becomes defined by nonintervention. It is claims such as these that help us identify paternalism as a threat to our individual autonomy. And we can see how these visions of autonomy and freedom as nonintervention produce a commitment to noninterference and so resist care as a public value.

We might be tempted to read Rawls's difference principle as a recognition of the problematic assumption of self-sufficiency and perhaps illustrative of a commitment to care as a public value. He does defend a redis-

tributive scheme and says it is necessary to meet needs.[2] But here needs are
met in order to ensure the liberal value of independence and autonomy;
certain social minimums are required in order to make such liberty possible. Meeting needs is a background condition for the primary public value
of individual freedom. The motivation for meeting needs is not particularistic attachment but rather a commitment to "maximize the long-run
expectations" of the least advantaged "consistent with the constraints of
equal liberty and fair equality of opportunity" (Rawls 1971, 277). As we
shall see, the place of needs in work on the ethic of care differs substantially.

Moreover, when we step back from the conversation about justice as it
takes place in the debates about care to think about the justice of American institutions, we can see that Rawls's vision of justice is largely eclipsed
by Locke's version. Rawls's idea that the veil of ignorance is appropriate to
deriving principles of justice as fairness is reflected in our political institutions — not least in the veil/blindfold of lady justice herself. But Locke's
equation of autonomy with economic self-sufficiency seems to have had a
more pervasive influence on our thinking about justice as is reflected in the
welfare reform debates cited in Chapter 1.

Care as an Alternative

Contemporary work on the ethic of care as an alternative to justice began
with a debate in moral psychology. For an overview of this debate, we will
start with an examination of the work of Carol Gilligan, using her dialogue with Lawrence Kohlberg to differentiate key aspects of "care" and
"justice" orientations toward moral reasoning. Returning to the work of
Kohlberg is important to understanding the nature of the challenge Gilligan is offering; it is critical to understanding the emphasis on both context

2. Rawls argues for the need for a transfer branch that takes needs into account and
assigns them an appropriate weight with respect to others' claims. "A competitive price system gives no consideration to needs and therefore it cannot be the sole device of distribution." He goes on, "From the standpoint of the legislative stage it is rational to insure oneself
and one's descendants against these contingencies of the market. Indeed, the difference principle presumably requires this. But once a suitable minimum is provided by transfers, it may be
perfectly fair that the rest of total income be settled by the price system." It is the fact that the
market is not suited to address needs that makes this transfer branch necessary (Rawls 1971,
276–77).

and attachment in the work on care. I want to examine Kohlberg's claims as well as those of Gilligan in order to make clear the points of departure.

Specifically, I am interested in contrasting these orientations along the lines of my analysis of Rawls. I want to explore three dynamics — the vision of the self in each orientation, the process of moral reasoning, and the transformation of moral reason into political practice — and to suggest important parallels between the debate about moral development in psychology and morality in political theory in order to draw out the political implications of each orientation. In particular, I will examine the relationship of Gilligan and Kohlberg to the liberal "justice" tradition. This tradition, as we have seen in the discussion of Rawls, has been defined by a common substantive commitment to personal liberty and a methodological commitment to the social contract (Kittay and Meyers 1987, 4). I will suggest what Gilligan's work might mean as a critique of these positions.

The ethic of care, conceptualized as an alternative to an ethic of justice, is usually attributed to Carol Gilligan's *In a Different Voice* ([1982] 1993). As Gilligan herself has noted, however, alternatives to an ethic of justice as Kant, Rawls, and, derivatively, Kohlberg understood it, have a much longer history — a history that includes David Hume, Adam Smith, and, some would argue, Jean-Jacques Rousseau. Key to characterizing this work as alternative to justice-oriented approaches to moral decision making is the move away from a rigid impartiality as the standard for moral decision making. Gilligan characterizes the ethic of care in the following terms:

> The distinction between justice and care as alternative perspectives or moral orientations is based empirically on the observation that a shift in the focus of attention from concerns about justice to concerns about care changes the definition of what constitutes a moral problem and leads the same situation to be seen in different ways. Theoretically, the distinction between justice and care cuts across the familiar divisions between thinking and feeling, egoism and altruism, theoretical and practical reasoning. It calls attention to the fact that all human relationships, public and private, can be characterized both in terms of equality and in terms of attachment and that both inequality and detachment constitute grounds for moral concern. Since everyone is vulnerable both to oppression and to abandonment, two moral visions — one of justice and one of care — recur in human experience. The moral injunctions, not to act un-

fairly toward others, and not to turn away from someone in need, capture these different concerns. (Gilligan 1987, 20)

The emphasis on "attachment" rather than impartiality, on vulnerability rather than autonomy, as the basis for moral concerns is critical to distinguishing the care orientation from the justice orientation. As the case studies illustrate, attentiveness to attachments, particularly communal attachment, is critical to understanding the practices of care. And as Chapters 4 and 5 illustrate, the tension between justice as impartiality and care as involving attachment also makes it problematic to bring justice and care frameworks together. The following section details Gilligan's challenge to Kohlberg's work, specifically focusing on the tension between impartiality and attachment as the basis for conceptualizing moral claims.

Gilligan and Kohlberg

Recently there has been a great deal of work developing the concept of care. I suggested earlier that the increasing concern to theorize an ethic of care as well as to model a practice of care is related to the fact that the work of care is increasingly performed within public rather than private settings. In this context the question of what a politics committed to care as a public value would look like is a newly legitimate topic of concern in policy and academic domains. Much of the recent work on care, women, and the welfare state is helpful in addressing this. It is often uniquely interdisciplinary in its approach to care, adopting and responding to work in psychology, sociology, and philosophy, as well as drawing on and influencing work within fields such as nursing and social work.

Yet what is also clear after examining this literature is that it would be difficult to capture the multiple meanings of "care," given the range of work on the topic. For this project, however, I think it is possible to begin our exploration of care with the work of five authors: Carol Gilligan's *In a Different Voice*; two works by Nel Noddings, *Caring: A Feminine Approach to Ethics* and *The Challenge to Care in Schools*; Joan Tronto's *Moral Boundaries*; Diemut Bubeck's *Care, Gender, and Justice*; and Selma Sevenhuijsen's *Citizenship and the Ethics of Care*. Gilligan's work is obviously critical; her work is widely read and is treated as representative of the "care" tradition. I have selected the latter works for discussion in

Chapter 4 because of their relevance for this particular project. Noddings, Tronto, Bubeck, and Sevenhuijsen are committed to thinking through the broader implications of care for institutional arrangements. Their respective approaches vary considerably, as will be detailed later in that chapter. In this sense, a contrast may demonstrate both the limitations and the potential of "care" as a guide for politics.

It would be difficult to overestimate the impact of Carol Gilligan's work, *In a Different Voice,* on the social sciences. Even those who are not immersed in contemporary feminist debate have become familiar with her challenge to traditional conceptualizations of moral development. While working with Lawrence Kohlberg, Gilligan became interested in expanding his studies of moral development to include female subjects. Though Kohlberg claimed universality for his stage theory of development, his original study assessed only the development of young men. Moreover, when his studies were expanded to include women, women consistently scored at stage three on a six-stage scale of development. Gilligan set out to explore the differences in the moral reasoning of men and women and ultimately theorized that the approach to moral reasoning was related to gendered experiences. She argues that it is ironic that "the very traits that traditionally have defined the 'goodness' of women, their care for and sensitivity to the needs of others, are those that mark them as deficient in moral development" (Gilligan [1982] 1993, 18).

In setting up a discussion of Gilligan's work, it is helpful to briefly review the aspects of Kohlberg's work that she was challenging. Influenced by Piaget, Kohlberg developed a theory of the stages of moral development. His model consisted of six stages that he grouped in pairs to form three levels. Kohlberg hypothesized that moral development is best described as moving from the preconventional to the conventional, and finally to the postconventional or "autonomous" stage.[3] The preconventional level is characterized by responsiveness to the labels "good" and "bad," but only because these terms have physical consequences such as punishment, reward, exchange of favors. At the second or conventional level, rules of an individual's family, group, or nation are perceived as valuable in their own right. There is a concern not only with conforming to the individual's social order but also with maintaining, supporting, and justifying this order. Finally, at the postconventional level, moral reasoning is

---

3. Kohlberg and Gilligan, "The Adolescent as a Philosopher" (1971), 1066. In-text references to Kohlberg that follow are to this work.

governed by a major thrust toward autonomous moral principles that have validity and application apart from the authority of groups or persons who hold them and apart from the individual's identification with those persons or groups. Kohlberg claims that these "cognitive-developmental stages" are stages that tell us *how* the individual thinks, not what he thinks about; and in this sense, Kohlberg claimed that his model had explanatory value across cultures.

I want to emphasize several aspects of his work here for the sake of comparison with Gilligan's. The postconventional stage is differentiated from the conventional by a commitment to moral principles that are universal, that have a claim to some nonrelative validity. It is exactly the perception of relativism—the awareness that "any given society's definition of right and wrong, however legitimate, is only one among many, both in fact and theory"—that precipitates the move from conventional to postconventional stages. Kohlberg describes Stage 6 as

> [o]rientation toward ethical principles appealing to logical comprehensiveness, universality, and consistency. These principles are abstract and ethical (the Golden Rule, the categorical imperative); they are not concrete moral rules like the Ten Commandments. Instead, they are universal principles of justice, of the reciprocity and equality of human rights, and of respect for the dignity of human beings as individual persons. (1068)

Kohlberg's theory of moral development asserts a relationship between Piaget's logical stages and his moral stages, arguing that the logical stages are a necessary but not sufficient condition for the attainment of corresponding moral stages. A critical question then arises: What more than movement through logical stages is required for movement through moral stages? Kohlberg says explicitly, "What is being asserted, then, is not that moral judgment stages are cognitive—they are not the mere application of logic to moral problems—but that the existence of moral stages implies that normal development has a basic cognitive-structural component" (1071). Yet, a comparison of Kohlberg's description of Piaget's stage theory and his own reveals some tight parallels. In describing the universal cognitive stages of Piaget, Kohlberg writes:

> [I]t is the transition from logical inference as a set of concrete operations to logical inference as a set of formal operations or "opera-

tions upon operations." "Operations upon Operations" imply that the adolescent can classify classification, that he can combine combinations, that he can relation relationships. It implies that he can think about thought, and create thought systems or "hypothetico-deductive" theories. This involves the logical construction of all possibilities — that is the awareness of the observed as only a subset of what may be logically possible. (1061)

And Kohlberg's description of movement in his own stage theory:

Each step of development then is a better cognitive organization than the one before it, one which takes account of everything present in the previous stage but making new distinctions and organizing them into a more comprehensive or more equilibrated structure. What is the relation of moral stage development in adolescence to cognitive stage development? In Piaget's and our view, both types of thought and types of valuing (or of feeling) are schemata which develop a set of general structural characteristics representing successive forms of psychological equilibrium. The equilibrium of affective and interpersonal schemata, justice or fairness, involves many of the same basic structural features as the equilibrium of cognitive schemata logicality. Justice (portrayed as balancing the scales) is a form of equilibrium between conflicting interpersonal claims, so that, "in contrast to a given rule imposed upon the child from outside, the rule of justice is an imminent condition of social relationships or a law governing their equilibrium." (1071)

The exact nature of the relationship between cognition and morality is not clear. What is clear is that moral development appears to be a subset of cognitive development and that this accounts in part for the parallel stage theories. On this model, "valuing" also appears to conform to the "general structural characteristics" of cognition. For all intents and purposes, the distinction between affect and cognition is collapsed, and affect is subsumed to cognition in this move. Given that Kohlberg defines stages as stages of structure and not of content, the question then remains, What is the difference between *how* the theoretical physicist thinks and *how* the principled moral reasoner thinks? Gilligan's answer to this question is in part that the difference *is* in the content of what is thought about; that is, how one thinks about theoretical physics versus how one thinks about moral questions is different because "Who are the actors?" and "What are their needs?" become relevant questions to ask when attempting to resolve moral dilemmas, whereas these questions are supposedly not relevant when one is thinking about physics. But to acknowledge that thinking about physics differs from thinking about morality because of the content of what is thought about is already to threaten the structure of moral reason as Kohlberg understands it, for it is this structure, apart from content, that is the source of his stage theory. At this point, I think it is possible to say something about Kohlberg's vision of the self, the process of moral reasoning, and the translation of moral reason into political practice. Kohlberg's postconventional stage is defined by an autonomous self — a self that most adequately thinks about moral questions when it is autonomous, totally separated or unattached to the actors in question, invoking not conventions, but rather higher order principles that transcend these conventions in order to reach resolution. Justice is not a condition imposed by social conventions "from the outside," but rather an "imminent condition of social relationships" themselves. Justice is seemingly generated on the basis of increasingly sophisticated cognitive organizational structures. What it is exactly that is being organized, the content, is not clear. But it is this commitment to thinking about justice as derived from a series of "operations upon operations" — securing the claims of justice by abstracting them from particular conventional political practice — that produces the hierarchically organized stage theory in which abstract human rights claims represent the most developed form of moral reasoning. Kohlberg himself portrays his highest stage of moral reasoning in the following terms: "Moving to a perspective outside of that of his society, he identifies morality with justice (fairness, rights, the Golden Rule), with recognition of the rights of others as these are defined naturally or intrinsically."[4]

Gilligan contrasts her own approach to Kohlberg's in very explicit terms:

> In this conception, the moral problem arises from conflicting responsibilities rather than from competing rights and requires for its resolution a mode of thinking that is contextual and narrative rather than formal and abstract. This conception of morality as concerned with the activity of care centers moral development around the understanding of responsibility and relationships just as

4. Cited in Gilligan 1993, 20.

the conception of morality as fairness ties moral development to the understanding of rights and rules. (Gilligan [1982] 1993, 19)

Kohlberg's version of justice has to be framed in the language of rights, for as Gilligan notes, he takes all constructions of responsibility to be merely conventional forms of moral reasoning. This is because responsibilities are supposedly particular in a way in which rights are not. Yet we might ask at this point, What makes "rights" more "universal" than responsibility? Is there not for every right a corresponding responsibility that we respect that right for others? In fact, this seems to be exactly what Kohlberg means when he calls the highest stages of moral reasoning "universal." Alternatively, we might ask, Why are "rights" viewed as any less "conventional" than "responsibilities"? Upon what foundations can Kohlberg make such a claim? I am not sure that there are foundations for such a claim, but by locating her study of moral development in the practices of moral decision making, Gilligan can avoid having to make such claims for either rights or responsibilities. By centering the caring approach to moral decision making in the *practices* of moral decision making, she leaves aside questions about the ontological status of rights claims and is, therefore, able to focus on the meaning of rights and responsibility in the practices, particularly of women's moral decision making.

Her first challenge is to Kohlberg's method of analyzing moral decision making, which tended to view those, again particularly but not exclusively women, who took a highly contextual approach to moral decision making as rooted in the conventional and therefore less highly developed as moral reasoners. In the course of assessment interviews designed to measure their stages of moral reasoning, many subjects felt they were given inadequate information for decision making and requested more information from interviewers before offering a response. They also tended to think of moral claims as highly situational and were less concerned to come up with a rule that governed all such situations than to focus on the needs of those presented in the dilemma. Again, contrasting one of her interviewees directly with Kohlberg's, Gilligan notes that "while Kohlberg's subject worries about people interfering with each other's rights, this woman worries about . . . the possibility of omission, of your not helping others when you could help them" ([1982] 1993, 21).

While the responses of women were not uniformly "care oriented," there was a notable correlation between gender and the care approach. How might we explain this? Gilligan hypothesizes that this more care-oriented approach to moral decision making has its origins in the experience of "women in man's life cycle." Relying on the work of Nancy Chodorow, she suggests that because women are the primary childcare providers in our society, they experience connection rather than separation as a primary part of their identity:

> Female identity formation takes place in a context of ongoing relationships since "mothers tend to experience their daughters as more like, and continuous with, themselves." Correspondingly, girls, in identifying themselves as female, experience themselves as like their mothers, thus fusing the experience of attachment with the process of identity formation. In contrast, "mothers experience their sons as a male opposite," and boys, in defining themselves as masculine, separate their mothers from themselves.[5]

Thus, when we turn to compare the vision of the self, the process of moral reasoning, and the connection to political practice in Gilligan's work with Kohlberg's, the question of gender is unavoidable. In part, Gilligan is documenting an empirical difference in moral orientation and claiming that masculine visions of the self differ from feminine visions of the self. Where does this then leave the process of moral decision making? Kohlberg might well say such differences are irrelevant to his claims about the hierarchy of moral decision making. Whatever the source of the difference between the reasoning of men and the reasoning of women on these subjects, he could still claim that the former is a more desirable, higher stage of reasoning. And in fact, his claims that "care" can be accommodated by his original framework seem to amount to just that; he can account for care as a conventional mode of reasoning. Kohlberg and Kramer (1969) suggest that if women are engaged professionally outside the home and occupy the same social position as do men, they too will reason at *higher* stages of moral development.

Within feminism, both academic and activist, Gilligan's work has come to represent a significant challenge to such conclusions and to liberal feminism more generally. For while Gilligan's work documents male versus female differences in the patterns of moral reasoning, she explicitly avoids a strategy that advocates that women "transcend difference from" and come

5. Chodorow quoted in Gilligan 1993, 8.

to reason like men. Rather, she articulates the purpose of her project in the following manner:

> In presenting excerpts from this work, I report research in progress whose aim is to provide in the field of human development a clearer representation of women's development which will enable psychologists and others to follow its course and understand some of the apparent puzzles it presents especially those that pertain to women's identity formation and their moral development in adolescence and adulthood. For women I hope this work will offer a representation of their thought that enables them to better see its integrity and validity, to recognize the experiences their thinking refracts and to understand the line of its development by using the group left out in the construction of theory to call attention to what is missing in its account. (Gilligan [1982] 1993, 3–4)

Gilligan's "agenda," then, might be understood as that of a researcher attempting to formulate a more complete theory; that is, a theory with more explanatory value, through the incorporation of a more complete sample of subjects. Yet by giving women's thought "validity," Gilligan means more than to suggest empirically verifying that "it is the case that" women often think in this alternative way; for Gilligan is not "ethically neutral" about the process of documenting this "different voice." She writes,

> [I]n the aftermath of the Holocaust and the Middle Passage, it is not tenable for psychologists or social scientists to adopt a position of ethical neutrality or cultural relativism—to say that one cannot say anything about values or that all values are culturally relative. Such a hands-off stance in the face of atrocity amounts to a kind of complicity. But the so-called objective position that Kohlberg and others espoused within the canon of traditional social science research was blind to the particularities of voice and the inevitable constructions that constitute point of view. However well-intentioned and provisionally useful it may have been, it was based on an inerrant neutrality which concealed power and falsified knowledge. (1993, xviii)

Gilligan, then, is clearly committed to revealing power and producing more accurate knowledge. But the criteria for what counts as relevant knowledge has also clearly shifted to a process of reasoning that takes into account particularity, not with an eye to generating abstract rules, but rather with an eye to meeting real needs.

Moral and Political Subjects

To what extent does the debate between Kohlberg and Gilligan in moral psychology have its parallels in political theory? I have contrasted Kohlberg and Gilligan with respect to aspects of their theories of moral development: the vision of the self, the process of moral reasoning. I turn now to the third point of contrast: the translation of moral reasoning into political practice. What are the implications of the contrasting visions of the self, and how has this vision of the self as moral subject been played out in political theory? We now move from the domain of moral and developmental psychology to work more explicitly focused on the moral reasoner as political subject.

Many feminist theorists have focused attention on the connections between Kant, Rawls, and Kohlberg and alternatively on parallels between Hume's work and Gilligan's argument. Kohlberg defines his version of justice as Kantian and commits to a categorical imperative to define the highest stages of moral reasoning. He also seems to fear, in the same way as did Kant, the contamination of morality by the empirical world. Kohlberg's emphasis on moving beyond conventions to universal principles resonates with the dominant philosophical view of morality handed down from Kant that "a moral theory should arise not out of the concrete circumstances of any given society, but out of the requirements of reason" (Tronto 1993, 9). Kant defines the domain of morality as exactly that which transcends the particularity of the sensible world. Kohlberg seems devoted to similar criteria when he describes the highest stage of moral reasoning in the following terms: "[It] is characterized by a major thrust toward autonomous moral principles which have validity and application apart from authority of the groups or persons who hold them and apart from the individual's identification with those persons or groups" (Kohlberg and Gilligan 1971, 1066–67). It is the location of justice outside of conventions that gives it its value as a standard for moral decision making.

Similarly, Annette Baier has argued that Hume's work displays certain consistencies with work on women and moral theory such as Gilligan's. Hume argues that when we contest the validity of moral claims, we do not contest them by invoking higher, more general rules. Rather, we test them against our ability to recognize and sympathetically share the reactions of others to that system of rights, to communicate feelings and understand what our fellows are feeling (Baier 1987, 41). Such a standard of morality requires actual content that it is exactly the project of Kohlberg and Kant to weed out.

Kant wrote to refute Hume. In light of this can we assume derivatively that where we have a commitment to justice this is incompatible with care? As we will see in the following chapters, feminist theorists such as Susan Okin, Seyla Benhabib, Joan Tronto, and Claudia Card have all expressed an unwillingness to give up on justice, to see it wholly replaced by care. And as Virginia Held has argued, such doubts make sense "since women so clearly need and deserve more justice and fairness than we have received in political life, on the job, at school and especially in the division of labor in the household" (Held 1995, 1–2). Justice is associated with an equality and respect for persons that for many very good reasons feminists want to hold on to.

However, Bonnie Honig's analysis of Kant suggests several reasons for concern about the compatibility of Kantian conceptions of justice with the orientation to care. She argues that despite Kant's commitment to respect for persons, respect for individuals as individuals, "Kantian respect is for the moral law, not for persons. At times, Kantian respect is for the morally worthy parts of persons, but it is never persons tout court; and it is certainly never for those who are other, only for the possibility of their conversion to moral worthiness" (Honig 1993, 18). In the terms I have been using, Honig seems to be arguing that Kantian respect is for abstract rather than actual persons.

Honig suggests this distinction between abstract and actual persons when she refers to Kant's visions of his moral subjects as "fables." And there is much about the Kantian fable of individualism that we have taken for granted in our own working vision of justice.[6] Kant's abstract persons are understood as properly moral subjects because of their autonomy, because of their self-sufficiency. Honig writes:

> Kant's account of Eden features a single, self-sufficient man paired
> with a woman (who is necessary for the reproduction of the species

6. See Mitchell 1998, especially chapters 1 and 2.

but not for anything else lest she compromises the self-sufficiency of man). . . . All of man's objective moral ends are pre-figured in this originary state: self-sufficiency (later to be transfigured to autonomy), the continuation of the species through propagation, a state of peace (although this peace is not yet perpetual because it is pre-rational) and sociability. (1993, 19–20)

On the Kantian account, self-sufficiency is integral to claims about autonomy and impartiality. Autonomy is a property of the wills of all adult human beings insofar as they are viewed as ideal moral legislators. This entails considering principles from a point of view that requires temporary detachment from the particular desires and aversions, loves and hates, that one happens to have. And as Thomas Hill notes, Kant called this "abstracting from personal differences" (1987, 131). Autonomy and impartiality then are integral to one another, and autonomy allows that basic moral principles are grounded in pure reason; independent of all contingent features of human nature, they admit no exceptions. Given the importance of autonomy to deriving right moral principles, it is easy to see why dependency would be threatening. But more important, as Honig notes, Kantian respect for this autonomy, for human beings as ends in themselves, is really a Kantian respect for human beings as the means to the end of the moral law.

Honig carefully distinguishes three distinct but overlapping senses in which Kant talks about respect for persons. In each of these cases, Honig argues, Kant's respect is not ultimately for actual people, for persons "tout court," but rather for the moral law as it is manifest in the actions and self-legislation of Kantian subjects. In the end, "The object of reverence is the law alone."[7] Moreover, while "respect" or "reverence" may be understood as feelings, Honig notes that it is important to recognize that respect or reverence for the law is not received through outside influence but is self-produced by a *rational* concept. In this way Kant maintains the purity of moral law by protecting its source from contamination.[8]

What is the significance of Honig's reading of Kant? She argues, I think persuasively, that Kant's respect for persons is a very bounded respect:

7. Kant quoted in Honig 1993, 27.
8. Annette Baier describes the Kantian version of morality this way: it "sees moral norms as carrying the authority of some divine reason whose job it is to issue laws which control but do not grow out of natural human sources of motivation." This is the aspect of Kant that resists the Humean account of morality (Baier 1985, 137).

"[T]he practice of respect that is famous for elevating and enshrining man as an end unto himself turns out to consist in the requirement that he order his behavior and his thoughts in conformity with certain moral ends."[9] And, she concludes,

[H]e depends on fables to make the world into a more secure home for man and to give him the faith he needs to participate in the collective and perpetual project of developing virtue in the species. The fables tell man that he is an end in himself, but along the way, means and ends are inverted. The construction of the home becomes the end, and man—the Kantian subject—a means to it. (Honig 1993, 40)

Ironically, given the value of autonomy, on this account it is possible to defend paternalism. For there is not the need to respect persons as such, but rather to respect persons whose behavior and thoughts are in conformity with certain moral ends. Those whose behaviors and thoughts are not in conformity with these ends need not be respected, and indeed may well be properly the subjects for intervention. Kant's move to metaphysics is exactly to prevent the infiltration of passions for particular others into the making of the laws. We must abstract from these affections in order to maintain the purity of moral law—so that our moral feelings are a product of a self-produced rational concept. Yet Hume's point is in part that the persuasive power of the law—our *motivation* to actually live in accordance with it—requires attention to the affections, because questions of motivation are always tied to these affections. Hume critiques those who want to locate moral distinctions in abstract reason alone: "There is an inconvenience which attends all abstruse reasoning, that it may silence without convincing an antagonist, and requires the same intense study to make us sensible of its force that was requisite for its invention" (1948, 31). Hume argues that to have moral law govern our behavior requires an account of motivation that admits the role of passion or affection.

Baier draws the parallels between Gilligan's work and Hume's position on several levels. Hume downplays the role of reason and plays up the role of feeling in moral judgment, emphasizing sympathy for others as the basis for our moral judgments: "To become a good fellow-person one doesn't

9. Honig 1993, 18. For an account of exactly how bounded Kantian respect for persons is, see Charles Mills, *The Racial Contract* (1997).

consult some book of rules, but cultivates one's capacity for sympathy or fellow feeling as well as for that judgment needed when conflicts arise between the different demands on us such sympathy may lead us to feel" (Baier 1987, 40).

Moreover, this motivating sympathy, by contrast with Kant's rationally based moral feelings, is shaped by convention, by the ways conventions construct our proximity to others. The women Gilligan studied saw morality as primarily a matter of responsibilities arising out of their attachment to others. And, Baier remarks, Hume, like Gilligan's subjects, "takes real problems in concrete historical settings, where the past history as well as the realistic future prospects for a given group are seen as relevant to their moral predicaments and their solutions" (1987, 47). So we have a comparable emphasis on moral subjects as actual persons in the work of Hume and Gilligan, and as abstract persons in Kohlberg and Honig's reading of Kant. The case studies suggest that the way those in the communities reason about their moral obligations is very much influenced by their attachments, their proximity, to others. Moreover, the motives of "outsiders" are always suspect. In this sense, Hume and Gilligan offer accounts of the workings of moral obligations that seem more helpful to understanding practice. Is it therefore a better guide to reorienting practice?

I believe it is, but I want to acknowledge two related problems that the Humean model of moral obligation presents—not surprisingly, work on care encounters comparable problems. The first is the problem of challenging attachments when those attachments produce a parochialism that is inconsistent with other political values. The second is the relationship between the motivation to care based on these attachments and the problem of knowing how to provide care.

Lawrence Mitchell presents an account of Hume's philosophy that illustrates the interconnection between these problems:

> [M]oral development relies on the similarities among people and their physical and situational proximity in the world. They [Hume and Smith] described the feeling this produces as "moral sympathy." It may be easier to understand the concept if you think of it as empathy, which comes closer in contemporary usage to what they meant. The term empathy is also free of the implications of pity that we often associate with sympathy in modern usage. The ideas are straightforward and intuitive. It is precisely what Bill Clinton means when he uses the phrase for which he is roundly mocked, "I

feel your pain." Think about how you react when you see another person in pain. Typically, we identify with that pain and, in a sense, feel it ourselves. Do you flinch when you see a particularly violent scene in a movie, or turn in horror when the evening news presents yet another person's tragedy? If so, you feel their pain in the sense that Clinton (and Hume and Smith) mean. If you do, you understand moral sympathy. (Mitchell 1998, 133)

He goes on to add, "We experience these reactions because the pain and happiness that others are experiencing are within our own experience as human beings. They are experiences that are common to us and part of what makes us human" (133). Mitchell's claims raise an interesting question: If moral sympathy is a result of experiences we share as human beings, why is it that we mock Clinton? Hume argues that sympathetic reactions are strongest with people closest to us emotionally and physically and that distance and separation make it much harder to cultivate these feelings of sympathy. I think we mock the president's claim because we are not persuaded that he *has* experienced our pain. We don't think he knows it experientially, and in light of this it is difficult to imagine that he feels it.

Hume introduced sympathy because he thought reason alone could offer us at best an inadequate account of moral obligation. It seems critical, however, to ask what exactly sympathy means as the basis for moral theory. If we are indeed most sympathetic to those we see as resembling ourselves, what are our obligations to those who are different and distant? If we are skeptical of Clinton's claim that he "feels our pain," does this imply too that we should be skeptical of his moral commitment to us?

Baier argues that while Hume does not believe reason alone can discern what is right, since reason is seen as always serving some sentiment or passion, reason does have a role to play. For in order for sentiments to count as moral sentiments, they must be "steady and general," arising from a reflective, reasoned consideration of the good of all concerned. In this way, certain sentiments have a capacity for enlargement by sympathetic spread and a need for built-in reinforcement from others, which through correction and adjustment of more partial sentiments can produce genuinely moral sentiment. This potential for "enlargement" may resist parochialism, a subject to which I will return in my final chapter. For now I want to focus on the way this process of enlargement illustrates the Humean subject as an actual alternative to the abstract subject of Kantian thought. In some sense the Humean subject is the subject "tout court" to which Honig refers, for she begins as an actual person with particular attachments that are renegotiated or reinforced in a process of reflective engagement with others.

Conclusion: The Ethic of Care and the Politics of Need

In much work on moral psychology, questions regarding the relationship between cognition and affect, knowledge and motivation, are framed as questions about individual psychological capacities. In keeping with the methodological approach of both Hume and Gilligan, I want to frame these questions within actual practices, with an emphasis on the political rather than psychological dimension, by locating them in the practices of public care. As the case studies demonstrate, what matters here is not so much what people's motivations in fact are, but whose motivations are trusted. What matters is not so much who is knowledgeable, but whose knowledge counts; that is, whose knowledge informs the process of re-source allocation. Both the New Futures and the Beacons programs illus-trated recipients expressing real skepticism about an ideal of disinterested knowledge on the part of providers. The Beacons staffers suggested that often traditional providers were motivated by a desire to play savior—to be able to say, "This is great, look at my program." But even where the motivations of "outsiders" to provide care were identified as benevolent, where there was evidence of a shared sense of distress, participants in New Futures and Beacons programs were skeptical that these motivations would lead to appropriate care. Many I spoke with in Savannah distrusted the parochialism of the "same 200." They were concerned about both their motives for involvement in collaboration and their ability to under-stand and therefore their authority to define need. The "experience that comes with living" was a critical foundation for trusting both motive and capacity to care appropriately. Simply put, a caring character was not ade-quate to getting the work of care done.

I close the chapter with one final question: If our central concern is developing a nonpaternalistic understanding of care, how is an "ethic of care" more or less adequate in addressing this concern?

The conventional paternalism critique is derivative of the assumptions of a justice-based approach to moral decision making. As such, I suggested in Chapter 1 that it is attentive to domination, but the basis of its critique of domination, "intervention in the lives of self-regarding others," assumes a norm of self-sufficiency that makes the practice of care itself unhelpfully problematic.

By contrast, as the comparison between Kohlberg and Gilligan illustrates, the "self-regarding" self is challenged in work on care. The substantive commitment to rights and obligations and the procedural commitment to fairness and impartiality that define the justice orientation are contrasted with an approach to moral reasoning that emerges out of particular relationships and is responsive to particular needs. Such an approach is compatible with care, but in its move away from rule-governed decision making, does it introduce the possibility of domination? Without some vision of the autonomous self, how can we resist, either conceptually or politically, relations of domination? When we move to an ethic centered on care, one that embraces a "relational" self rather than an "autonomous" self, do we lose our ability to criticize relations, specifically relations of domination? And if not, what becomes the basis of our critique of domination? It can't be, at least not without substantial modification, unjustified "intervention in the lives of self-regarding others." On what basis can we resist relationships of domination?

The risks of such domination are quite real. Both case studies suggest that recipients were aware of such risks and often opted out of conventional organizations of public care to avoid them. Where care positions itself as a "professional" rather than a "political" activity, caregivers are often unable to see themselves as participating in a process that involves domination. They are focused on "real" needs, which they are trained both to discover and to address. As the professional-client relationships of New Futures illustrate, this is particularly true where needs themselves and the role of the caregiver are taken for granted rather than negotiated in the course of a democratic process.

Care in such a depoliticized context risks becoming a justification for unself-consciously defining the needs of others. This is particularly true of models of care that assume "care" is a matter of experts' discovering needs and designing efficient means for meeting them. I describe this process as un*self*-conscious quite purposefully, for in many ways, such a model of care assumes that the identity of those making knowledge claims (their selfhood) and their disposition toward those in need are irrelevant. Yet even models of care that appear to challenge such a distanced, rule-governed process of meeting needs may be problematic. Where care is derivative of empathy, and empathy is understood as "receiving the other into myself," relationships—and sometimes relationships of domination—become difficult to see. But they are often there. As Lorraine Code notes, "[T]he location of empathetic knowing in a professional setting produces power asymmetries that can turn this ideally reciprocal, mutually affirming skill into an imperialistic, coercive practice" (1995, 137). Where caring for others or knowing their needs are seen as either natural activities or matters of expertise, the empathizer or the knowing expert is allowed to forget him- or herself as relevant to the process of "caring" or "knowing"; he or she is allowed to forget that both caring and knowing are acts of interpretation in which the caregiver or the knower are active interpreters. The provider of care transcends his or her own particularity or contingency and thereby reads empathically caring or scientifically assessing the needs of others as apolitical; naturalizing both the role of care providers and the process of caretaking contributes to the sense that our organization of care is inevitable. In this context, the critique of domination seems irrelevant.

If we begin with a conception of needs as produced and interpreted within a social and political structure, we might also begin to rethink our understanding of domination. Rather than seeing it as a violation of autonomy or self-regardingness, participation in the process of defining needs could become the criteria by which we determine domination. When the authority in this process is located within a class of experts, it would evolve into paternalistic care; and in so doing, it would violate our democratic commitments to equal voice. However, when those who are in need participate in this process of defining needs, this would create a politics of needs interpretation appropriate to our democratic commitments. Furthermore, such participation would open up the space for conflict about what exactly is needed. As the case study of New Futures demonstrated, the conventional process of professional needs assessment may be criticized as both paternalistic and ineffective at meeting needs.

In the following chapters, we will examine alternatives to conventional conceptions of care. These alternatives suggest a complementary rather than contradictory relationship between justice and care. So formulated, might the problems suggested here be addressed if care were modified by an appropriate relationship to justice? It is to this question that we turn next.

4

Is Caring Ever Unjust?

In Chapter 2 we examined the practices of care as they unfolded in two collaborative attempts to reorganize social services. An analysis of the practices of New Futures suggested that there was a critical disparity between the needs of recipients as defined by professionals and the recipients' own articulation of their needs. I argued that in this case the politics of the process of needs interpretation works to reproduce the relationship of provider and recipient so that the authority of the provider to define needs remains largely unchallenged. The politics of defining needs in this way contributed to the failure to meet New Futures' outcome goals as defined by policy makers and worked to prevent the expression and actualization by recipients of an agenda more appropriate to their own needs. Chapter 3 gave a brief introduction to the ethic of care and set up the problem of interpreting needs within this framework. Finding that conceptual work on care is often inadequately attentive to the politics of this process, I argued that such inattentiveness tended to produce paternalistic practices of public care.

How do we remedy this both conceptually and politically? This chapter suggests what this case study might mean for the debate about the relationship of justice to care. We begin by asking whether the ethic of care alone can provide an adequate guide to public practices. A look at Nel Noddings's attempt at an institutional argument based in an ethic of care suggests that she leaves unaddressed both the problem of paternalism and the problem of parochialism, the neglect of strangers. We then examine attempts by several others to bring justice and care together. These attempts are prompted, as Claudia Card puts it, by the concern that care by itself cannot prevent evil (1990, 101).

I am interested in two questions. First, Is caring ever unjust? Specifically, Does "injustice" identify the problems with care? I have already suggested that justice orientations allow us to identify the problem of domination but that where domination is framed as a violation of autonomy understood as self-sufficiency, the critique of paternalism seems to require giving up care altogether. Thus, the second question that is a focus of this chapter: Is there an alternative formulation of justice and its relationship to care such that the standards of justice can be brought to the practices of care to improve them (to address both domination and neglect) rather than abandon them? Such a formulation presents real difficulties because care and justice, as Chapter 3 illustrated, rest on very different, often conflicting assumptions about how "good" and "bad" practices are determined; therefore, efforts to bring justice and care together often produce unworkable conceptual alternatives.

Ultimately, I will argue that the critical problems of care as a political practice are inadequately dealt with in most attempts to bring together justice and care. The pursuit of fairness as the remedy for either domination or neglect most often turns to a model of distributive justice that treats care as a good. As the case studies demonstrate, however, the practices of care, of meeting needs, are processes in which the identities of actors, the community context, and the prospects for trust seem to matter a great deal. Thus, when we treat care as a good, when we commodify it in order to reallocate it more fairly, we fail to recognize much of what is important to getting the work of care done. In order to appropriately meet needs, the case studies suggest that the particular identities of actors involved must be taken into account. But as Sevenhuijsen has noted, with distributive justice comes the baggage of equality-as-sameness (1998, 40). On this account of equality, we tend to see the differences that make particularity relevant as either deviant, in which case paternalistic care is justified, or natural, in which case the parochialism of care seems inevitable. This does not mean, however, that justice can have no role to play in shaping appropriate practices of public care. However, if we are to turn to justice in order to ensure the fairness of care, we must have a model of justice that can recognize care as a process rather than a commodity, that can acknowledge the particular identities of those involved in this process as relevant to appropriate care while simultaneously seeing the "us versus them" as a product of social and political practices that can be reconstructed to address concerns of parochialism. This is a substantially modified version of justice.

Justice and Care—Complementary or Contradictory?

I want to begin by pointing, very briefly, to the problem of bringing justice, as it is embodied in the conventional version of paternalism, together with care. I would argue that in its present formulation, nonpaternalism precludes the possibility of caring relationships. In thinking about the problem of paternalism in its familiar version, the relationship between justice and care is of critical importance. Paternalism here might be used to describe, for example, the intervention of service providers in the lives of self-regarding recipients and so would name a form of rights violation. Yet many of these interventions do not constitute a violation of formal rights. If we broaden the concept of "intervention" so that it includes interactions beyond those understood in terms of formal rights, the conventional/libertarian version of paternalism rapidly comes to justify withdrawing public social provision altogether. Because paternalism here is defined as "intervention in the lives of self-regarding others," collective responsibility is viewed with skepticism as "really" about the expression of the self-regarding interests of some over others — for what else could it be? It becomes difficult to see anything but "self-interest" at work here. But in order to prevent the self-regarding interests of some from dominating others, some neoliberals seem willing to neglect the place of "needs" altogether. In other words, correcting for paternalism by reference to justice seems to require us to give up care. Does this suggest a general incompatibility, or is the problem of paternalism unique?

Much of the more recent work on the "ethic of care" has argued that a positive caring relationship must be located within the context of justice, that care alone may simply not do the job. As Claudia Card queries, "Can an ethic of care without justice enable us to adequately resist evil?" (1990, 101). The arguments vary, and we will review some of them in this chapter. Common claims include: (1) while care may make a strong governing principle for personal relations, we need justice to ensure right treatment of the stranger (Card 1990); (2) (a variation on one) a care orientation may govern our personal interactions, but our public interactions require a justice orientation; (3) we need justice to guide our allocation of care (Tronto 1993; Bubeck 1995); (4) care should define our relationship to others, but "rights" create the space for the inclusion of the "self" in the network of care (Gilligan 1988); (5) we need justice in order to move beyond the particularity of care (Benhabib 1987); and (6) a reversal, justice needs care because justice requires the empathy of care in order to generate its principles (Okin 1990).

In this chapter I will focus on the political impetus for raising concerns about injustice within the theories and practices of care. I will leave the discussion of the place of care within theories of justice, a discussion that focuses on the work of Susan Okin and Robert Solomon, to the following chapter. I raise some questions here about the workability of frameworks that bring justice and care together, arguing that they are often not attentive enough to problems of compatibility that follow from defining the frameworks in opposition to one another.

Though each of these attempts to merge justice and care presents its own dilemmas, the authors raise important and difficult questions about the potential and limitations of theoretical work on care as a model for practice. How might we understand or interpret the case studies presented in the previous chapter in light of the relationship between justice and care as it has been variously formulated? In what terms do we understand its failure? How would we redesign such a program for greater success? How does conceptualizing the practical dilemmas involved in redesigning programs suggest directions for reconceptualizing the theoretical frameworks for care and justice? Over the course of the next three chapters, I hope to offer some insight into these questions.

Let us begin by recalling several aspects of the case studies that seem critical. First, there seemed to be a strong sense on the part of caregivers in the form of case managers, social workers, and Foundation personnel that the motivation for their involvement in this effort was that they "cared" about what happens to kids and families "at risk."[1] Second, many recipients we spoke with expressed a skepticism about "care" as the motivation and instead offered explanations like "They do it because it's their job," or "They want to keep us down." The case study of New Futures documented the lack of participation of recipients and the conflicting worldviews of bureaucrats in relation to families designated "at risk" and their advocates. In this case, does it make sense to ask who is right? And if those who receive services are correct, and providers and recipients "live in different worlds and speak different languages," is it possible to practice care across these differences? Would justice be necessary to doing so?

These are difficult questions, and their relevance is not isolated to this particular case study. Dempsey and Noblit (1996) argued in the course of historical work on southern schools that the move toward "justice" — that is, the move to integrate segregated schools — ultimately produced school environments that many black parents he interviewed believe are far less caring than the segregated schools they attended. Jan VanGalen (1996) has found evidence of injustice in school environments that teachers, administrators, parents, and students almost all understand as "caring." She points to the sexism and racism on the part of school authorities and, in light of this, asks, "What does it mean to call this environment caring?"

The debate that supposes an irreconcilable divide between justice and care has a difficult time understanding these questions, let alone suggesting their answers. To return to the vision of justice and care presented in Chapter 3, the argument that *justice* and *care* are oppositional terms, the former embodying impartiality, general principles, and universality; the latter, partiality, context, and particularity, makes the claim of "unjust caring" seem nonsensical. Of course care is not just — it is exactly the opposite. In some sense, both care and injustice have been formulated in opposition to justice. The harder question then becomes how we understand the

---

1. Joan Tronto's *Moral Boundaries* (1993) argues for the importance of distinguishing between four "analytically separate but interconnected phases of caring." Her distinction between caring about, and actually directly meeting, needs in the process of caregiving is relevant to differentiating what Foundation personnel meant when they claimed to "care" versus what advocates meant when they made the same claim. I will argue in the next two chapters that case managers were politicized advocates in part because of their role in caregiving rather than merely "caring about."

relationship between care and *in*justice. Where care has failed—that is, where the needs of the assumed subjects of intervention have not been met—it is the result of a lack of care. The invocation of justice or injustice is simply nonsensical here, for we need have no recourse to the values of justice (impartiality, general principles, etc.); and in fact, by proclaiming care as our goal, justice, it would seem, becomes irrelevant. Where justice and care are understood as antithetical to one another, there may be a failure of care, but it would have little to do with a failure of justice. Similarly, injustice could not be spoken of as a failure to care exactly because if justice is the desired outcome, care would have little to do with it, and in fact *should* have little to do with it.

The argument that care is an ethic for certain spheres and justice for others raises similar questions of compatibility. From where do we derive our understanding of the boundaries of these spheres? Or alternatively, how do we come to understand friend versus stranger? Are these boundaries drawn derivatively from the application of abstract principles, or are they constructed in the course of practice—and if the latter, can it also be the former? It becomes difficult to see how we can make justice and care compatible in some way that protects the impartiality of justice. Can justice be the governing principle of a sphere, the boundaries of which are established through the extension or limitation of affective ties? Would we still call this justice if "impartiality" has a circumscribed community to which it applies? In this chapter some of the responses that have been offered to these questions are outlined in greater detail in work on the ethic of care. In the chapter that follows, we will approach similar questions but begin with the ethic of justice. Taken together, these two chapters illustrate some of the difficulties of bringing justice and care together, while simultaneously acknowledging the inadequacy of either framework taken alone.

A critical aspect of this work is its attempt to formulate a complementary relationship between justice and care, which is, as I have suggested, often motivated by the concern to avoid domination in the process of care. Thus, this work attempts to more directly address political concerns. As I will suggest over the course of the next two chapters, there are some important parallels between the role of empathy in relation to politics and the political function performed by tacit reasoned consent in justice frameworks. Empathy becomes a way of knowing "good care," as abstract reason was the way to arrive at "right principles" of justice. Empathy, on several formulations, carries with it many of the risks of tacit consent in the justice tradition: it forecloses the active critical participation of the subject of consent or of care. A version of care based on such an understanding of empathy cannot serve as the basis for a process-oriented politics sensitive to issues of identity and their intersection with authority and domination. Ultimately, I will argue that a more adequate version of care requires a democratic process of needs interpretation for which neither the imagined needs nor the hypothetical consent of recipients of care substitute.

Gilligan's Version of Care: Supplement or Substitute for Kohlberg's Justice?

The irreconcilability of justice and care is suggested by several works on care, most notably the work of Nel Noddings. But in beginning with Gilligan's work, we begin with a less clear-cut case. Noddings builds on an understanding of Gilligan's work that depicts the relationship between justice and care as one of opposition. But because Gilligan's understanding of this opposition is complicated, let us begin by laying out several of the descriptions she offers in her attempt to articulate the exact nature of the relationship of care to justice.

Gilligan contrasts care and justice orientations throughout *In a Different Voice* ([1982] 1993), yet she frequently depicts them both as simultaneously oppositional and as mutually necessary to one another. She writes of care:

> In this conception, the moral problem arises from conflicting responsibilities rather than from competing rights and requires for its resolution a mode of thinking that is contextual and narrative rather than formal and abstract. This conception of morality as concerned with the activity of care centers moral development around the understanding of responsibility and relationships, just as the conception of morality as fairness ties moral development to understanding right and rules. (19)

Care is about responsibilities rather than rights, engagement rather than abstraction, connection rather than separation; it presumes the centrality of relationship rather than individualism. In some sense, Gilligan's seems to be a move that simply turns the justice orientation on its head; care seems to be the opposite, the inverse of justice. But I think this reading would miss some important aspects of care as an orientation, for in beginning with a focus on responsibilities rather than rights, on relationships rather than individualism, the care orientation redefines many of the dichotomies that stabilized the opposition of justice to care. Responsibility, for example, is conceptualized differently within the care framework: "Responsibility signifies response, an extension rather than a limitation upon one's actions" (38). Terms such as *responsibility* become about the extension of relationship rather than a limitation on individual freedom. Thus, it is not simply that care focuses on responsibility *rather than* rights, but that prioritizing responsibility actually requires an altered understanding of both responsibility and rights. In *In a Different Voice*, Gilligan suggests some of the communication dilemmas produced by such altered understandings:

> My research suggests that men and women may speak different languages that they assume are the same, using similar words to encode disparate experiences of self and social relationships. Because these languages share an overlapping moral vocabulary, they contain a propensity for systematic mistranslation, creating misunderstandings which impede communication and limit the potential for cooperation and care in relationships. At the same time, however, these languages articulate with one another in critical ways. Just as the language of responsibilities provides a web-like imagery of relationships to replace a hierarchical ordering that dissolves with the coming of equality, so the language of rights underlines the importance of including in the network of care not only the other but also the self. (173)

The web-like imagery of relationships becomes a backdrop for assertions of rights, and this has marked implications for the meaning of rights in social practice. It seems that rights in their reconstituted version within care may no longer sustain as legitimate the assertion of individual departures or exit from relationship. In a more recent work, *Mapping the Moral Domain* (1988), Gilligan suggests exactly this. She situates the "care" orientation in relation to Albert Hirschmann's framework for exit and voice in his 1970 work *Exit, Voice and Loyalty*. Gilligan argues that one implication of care is that Hirschmann's "exit" is not a legitimate option. The "caring" voice is one that is enmeshed in relationships and that recognizes the "messy" option of voice over the "clean" option of exit when conflict occurs. Gilligan asserts that with care, voice is still possible in the face of conflict, whereas with justice, exit is more likely to be the option. This seems an important insight. First, in political practice exiting a situation of conflict altogether is rarely an option, so messy options are what we are left with. Yet she seems to assume that it is clear why the messy option of conversation rather than the clean option of exit is desirable. As critics of care have suggested, this is not self-evidently the case. Gilligan seems to assume a terrain of equality in which speaking and being heard and responded to are necessary products of web-like relationships.

I raise a question here to which I will return repeatedly; that is, Why is it that a "relational" approach to moral problem solving, as well as to political dilemmas, is desirable? Why is messy better than clean? Gilligan compares justice and care as ordering principles of social relationships, arguing, "Whereas the rights conception of morality that informs Kohlberg's principled level (stages 5 & 6) is geared to arriving at an objectively fair or just resolution to moral dilemmas upon which all rational persons could agree, the responsibility conception focuses instead on the limitations of any particular resolution and describes the conflicts that remain" ([1982] 1993, 22).

This contrast illuminates a difference in moral conceptions without developing clearly the social consequences of this difference. Why, from the perspective of social consequences, is a focus on "the conflicts that remain" to be preferred? The assumption seems to be that the benefit of a messy approach is that the conflicts that remain theoretically remain on the table. That is, the focus is as much on disagreement as on agreement. On this account, disagreements are not "silenced without convincing an antagonist" (Hume 1948, 31). There is some clear evidence in the case studies that a rational bureaucratic process did exactly this. Outside experts, albeit often unintentionally, silenced recipients without convincing them either of their expertise or of their good intentions.

The ethic of care with its focus on voice may appear to avoid the problem of silence, the problem of domination. The assumption that the language of responsibility with its "web-like imagery of relationships . . . replaces a hierarchical ordering that dissolves with the coming of equality" contributes to this appearance. But without situating the question relationally—that is, Who is speaking for whom? To which groups are they speaking?—voice may be simply one form of self-expression rather than an act of deliberation among interdependent equals. Relationality does not by itself guarantee equality, nor is it a bulwark against paternalism; for the equality of web-like relationships requires not only attention to Gilligan's voice but also attention to the question of who is listening.

A relational approach to moral problem solving as well as to political dilemmas is desirable because it is a necessary though not sufficient prerequisite for a democratic politics of care. The "not sufficient" part is evidenced in the case study, for voice may be relational in its attempt to communicate, but the success of this communication is contingent on more than the intention of the speaker: the social positioning of listeners is important too. Some voices are louder than others, easier to hear, speaking in a language that resonates with the status quo. Others challenge the language of the status quo and therefore are more difficult to hear.[2] As one New Futures case manager described the experience of voice: "It's like we're from different worlds, speaking different languages." If voice is taken to be relational, we must explore the process of hearing too. In important ways, those who designed New Futures understood this, thus their emphasis on getting those with recognized authority on board. But as I suggested in my earlier analysis, planners assumed that the authority of bureaucrats, city managers, and superintendents would translate across community boundaries. The case studies suggest that it does not.

Authority must be contextualized, understood as implying a community of recognition. If those who speak feel they are treated as though they "don't know what they're talking about," voice may be of little comfort. Consequently, "exit" may be desirable even if difficult to achieve. This was clearly the opinion of several members of the Savannah-based group Guardians of the Culture. They had some formal opportunities for voice on the collaborative, but feeling they weren't being heard, they sought support from outside groups like the NEA; they in effect exercised an exit option. Gilligan and others who focus on voice often seem to assume that voice gets both heard and responded to, but this requires moves beyond the mere assertion of relationality to considerations of relationships of power and politics within and across community boundaries.

2. As Susan Bickford (1996) has noted, a theory not only of "voice" but of listening is central to developing a democratic theory. I return to her argument in greater detail in Chapters 6 and 7.

Care Without Justice: Noddings's Approach

In drawing a contrast between Noddings and Gilligan, it may help to review what they see "care" accomplishing in relation to their own work. Gilligan's work was quite directly a response to the work of Lawrence Kohlberg, seeking to explain why men fairly consistently outscored women on his scale of moral development. Gilligan explores the process of moral reasoning in relation to concrete moral dilemmas and finds a difference between men and women in the way they frame moral dilemmas. But her challenge to Kohlberg is not simply in noting that difference, for his own work documents a difference as well. Her challenge is in suggesting that the care orientation she uncovers is exactly that, an orientation, a framework, independent of justice, that is not assimilable to Kohlberg's stage theory. Furthermore, she argues that this approach to moral dilemmas has value. She need not claim that it necessarily has more value than justice. Yet the exact nature of the relationship between justice and care remains a bit unclear. On the one hand, the care framework seems to have a fundamentally different vision of the self at its core than does the justice orientation. This is a point that Gilligan develops quite explicitly. Yet she also claims that the language of rights can facilitate the inclusion of the caring self into networks of care. But rights here must substantially change meaning, for it is not clear that the language of rights works with selves who reason, not impartially, but in an attached fashion. Rights seem to be designed for the express purpose of preventing things like attachment from being factored into politics. Thus, Gilligan seems to concede the irreconcilability of the underlying assumptions about selfhood in these two orientations, while simultaneously claiming their mutual necessity to one another.

By contrast, Nel Noddings (1984) begins by challenging the adequacy of a justice orientation in the following terms:

> When we look clear-eyed at the world today, we see it racked with fighting, killing, vandalism, and psychic pain of all sorts. One of the saddest features of this picture of violence is that the deeds are so often done in the name of principle. When we establish a principle forbidding killing, we also establish principles describing the exceptions to the first principle. Supposing, then, that we are moral (we

are principled, are we not?), we may tear into others whose beliefs or behaviors differ from ours with the promise of ultimate vindication. (2)

Whereas Gilligan's position on the value of "care" is complicated by the fact that she is attempting to speak within the social scientific tradition, Noddings's position is much more explicitly normative. About a justice orientation she writes:

> Everything depends upon the nature and strength of this [caring] ideal, for we shall not have absolute principles to guide us. Indeed, I shall reject ethics of principle as ambiguous and unstable. Wherever there is a principle, there is implied its exception and too often, principles function to separate us from each other. We may become dangerously self-righteous when we perceive ourselves as holding a precious principle not held by the other. The other may be devalued and treated "differently." (5)

There are several key points made here. First, the analysis of principled approaches as self-righteous implies a critique from outside and not from within the principled approach to moral dilemmas. For it is, as I noted in Chapter 3, a critical characteristic of justice that it forgets the self as relevant to the process of moral reasoning—a literal lack of self-consciousness.[3] This may seem self-evident, and I am sure Noddings would agree. But it raises the practical dilemma of how this critique from outside the justice paradigm can speak to and modify it. Isn't it quite likely to be met with the response by the adherent to principle that this has nothing whatsoever to do with "self-righteousness" but only with "right" itself?

Second, it will strike many readers as ironic that Noddings actually sees the justice orientation as potentially devaluing others because of its emphasis on *difference*. Justice is commonly associated with sameness (the sameness achieved through the abstraction from concrete differences to the autonomy of moral reason), that is, the applicability of the same principle in the same way across everyone or at least every member of the just community. And this may be exactly Noddings's point: those who are not

3. As I suggested in the previous chapter, Rawls's depiction of the original position is constructed so that a "veil of ignorance" prevents each of us as individuals from knowing the self that we are or the position we hold in society. It is in the absence of such knowledge about the self that we are, according to Rawls, able to devise principles of justice as fairness.

members of the just community, where membership is formally defined in terms of sharing a set of principles, are not subject to the same treatment. This is, I think, more controversial than Noddings recognizes, for there are plenty of ways in which advocates of justice expect justice to govern all our relations, even relations with those who don't seem to share these principles of justice. It is exactly one of the characteristics of justice that it is claimed to be universalizable. But it is often the application of these principles of justice to those in positions of disadvantage that further disadvantages them. It is not so much that justice explicitly formulates its exceptions thus creating the space for injustice. Rather, it is the universal application of a single principle across quite different sets of material conditions that often results in devaluing.

A criticism perhaps more directly relevant to our analysis of the practices of public care is raised by Claudia Card (1990, 101). Card worries that it is Noddings's conception of care and its use of difference and distinction to delineate obligation that is problematic. Card makes reference to what has been a very controversial section of Noddings's argument:

> Our obligation is limited and delimited by relation. We are never free, in the human domain, to abandon our preparedness to care; but, practically, if we are meeting those in our inner circles adequately as ones caring and receiving those linked to our inner circles by formal chains of relation, we shall limit the calls upon our obligation quite naturally. We are not obliged to summon the "I must" if there is not possibility of completion in the other. I am not obliged to care for starving children in Africa, because there is no way for this caring to be completed in the other unless I abandon the caring to which I am obligated. I may still choose to do something in the direction of caring, but I am not obliged to do so. (Noddings 1984, 86)

The opposition of choice and obligation is quite purposeful here, and it is helpful to explore the roots of this opposition in Noddings's argument. Noddings derives her understanding of obligation from a notion of natural caring. She argues that morality, and by extension moral obligation, requires *feelings*, as opposed to principled reasons. It requires first the sentiment of natural caring, which she distinguishes from ethical caring by writing, "In situations where we act on behalf of the other because we want to do so, we are acting in accord with natural caring. A mother's caretaking efforts on behalf of her child are not usually considered ethical but natural" (1984, 79). As many others have pointed out, the mother-child relationship is a problematic place from which to begin thinking about public care. First, it presumes a natural or taken-for-granted relationship of authority in the context of care, where the appropriate model of political authority is conventional. It also maps dependency on to the model of care and takes for granted an inequality between caretaker and cared-for. Parental care is not an appropriate model for public care because we do not want to treat fellow citizens in need of care as though they are incompetent children. Noddings's model of care seems to assume that paternalistic relationships in the context of care are inevitable.

Taken together with her argument about circles of care, the mother-child model seems to create the justification for caring only for those in the inner circle, because such circles are somehow "natural." That is, those we prefer to care for, we must prefer to care for because of some natural affective tie; and these ties should guide our sense of moral obligation. Noddings's formulation raises several further concerns. First, the assertion that a mother's caretaking is natural rather than a product of gendered role socialization seems at the very least debatable. Noddings uses the mother-child relationship consistently throughout her work to illustrate caring. Indeed, she labels her "feminine approach to ethics" the approach of the mother in contrast with the detached role of the father. But even were we to accept some kind of biologically based caring sentiment between mother and child, we would still be left with the question of how we expand this caring to an "inner circle." Likewise, we would be left with the critical question of how we understand who is a member of this inner circle and who is not. Is such an understanding natural too?

Noddings's response to this first question is not clear-cut. She seems to want to say that the sentiment necessary to moral obligation is derivative of the natural sentiment to care. She argues that it is our remembrances of the natural caregiving in our earliest years that is the basis for an "I must" in response to the plight of another. But as opposed to the first instance of natural caring, ethical caring requires an effort; one must work to recall those memories as a guide to conduct. What prompts such an effort? To whose "plight" are we responsive? It is clear that in the practices of care, these are the critical questions. It is equally clear that they can be answered only with very specific information about the broader social and political context in which the practices of care unfold.

Moreover, the question of how the decision is made—for it is a "choice" here, as opposed to something natural, as to whom we extend care—is left largely undeveloped. Thus, when later on in this chapter Noddings asserts rather unproblematically that we have no obligation to care for the starving in Africa, it seems not clearly derivative from her argument. If it is the case that our obligations are limited and delimited by relationship, are we not in turn obliged to examine what counts as a relationship, the basis for this claim, and whether we may be "obligated" to expand our relations? Noddings skirts this question by asserting that "the very wellspring of ethical behavior is in human affective response," then adding,

> This does not mean that our discussion will bog down in sentiment, but it is necessary to give appropriate attention and credit to the affective foundation of existence. Indeed, one who attempts to ignore or to climb above the human affect at the heart of ethicality may well be guilty of romantic rationalism. What is recommended in such a framework simply cannot be broadly applied in the actual world. (1984, 3)

While I am sympathetic to Noddings's insistence that we not ignore the role of affective ties, it is not clear what exactly constitutes "appropriate attention" without "getting bogged down" in sentiment. In the discussion cited above, obligation seems to get reduced to existing between those to whom we feel affective ties, where affective ties are taken to be primarily or derivatively natural.

The potential for parochialism, for exclusivity, seems disturbing enough to prompt longing for the "romantic rationalism" that Noddings dismisses. Claudia Card asks the question, "Is care without justice adequate to enable us to resist evil?" I am inclined to agree with Card that in Noddings's version of care, care alone is not adequate to resisting "evil." This, as suggested at the opening of this chapter, is a critical question if we are to take care seriously as a guide for practices of the welfare state. Take for example the dilemma that might arise if those with resources (for simplification, say material resources) feel no affective ties to those without. Do we relieve the haves of any obligation to the have-nots just because they don't "feel" it? Noddings's response to the question of whether we are obliged to care for the starving in Africa seems to be that we are not. But here she makes the argument that we are *not* obligated because it would force us to abandon the "caring" to which we *are* obligated. It is a difficult practical issue, and one to be taken seriously, for as Noddings points out, we cannot care adequately for everyone. But the question of how we become obligated to care for some and not for "others" seems relevant and largely unanswered in Noddings's work. It is clear from the case studies that caring across the "we versus they" divide is complicated: not to recognize these boundaries is to ignore a variable critical to effective policy. But to naturalize the boundaries of these communities is as dangerous as ignoring them, particularly if, as Noddings concludes, such boundaries circumscribe the community for which we are obligated to care.

We must have a model of care that can both recognize such boundaries as relevant to care and provide the space for critical reflection on how these boundaries have been constructed through social and political practices (a history of foundation efforts that only get the community "halfway," for example) and so might be reconstructed. A beginning step in this direction, then, must be a recognition of care as a practice and a politics.

Care as a Politics: Getting the Work of Care Done

Joan Tronto offers one of the first, and certainly the most comprehensive, considerations of care as a politics. Given this, her work provides some critical contributions to my own thinking about care. In part this is a function of the disciplinary background that she brings to the question of care. Gilligan's concern is first and foremost to legitimate the way women approach moral dilemmas within the field of moral development psychology. As such, her work is concerned with the ordering of social relationships. Noddings comes to the debate about care with a background in philosophy and math education. Her work on moral education and her outline of the practice of care in schools are both largely theoretical pieces in which practices are not recommended, or where they are they seem difficult to actualize in the institutional context she assumes. This is somewhat ironic since what distinguishes "a feminine approach to ethics" from traditional approaches is supposedly its engagement with the actual. But Noddings seems to make "affect" a substitute for "actual" and moves on to spend most of her work theorizing about affect rather than dealing with the practical and political problems and potentials of affect for care. Tronto, as a political theorist, is committed to exploring and providing a prescriptive framework for the politics of care in practice.

This focus is facilitated by the fact that early on in *Moral Boundaries* (1993) she challenges the traditional boundary between the moral and the political. This is, I think, a critical first step in addressing the work of care not merely theoretically but practically, since in challenging this boundary, we also challenge traditional conceptions of care as moral and therefore, on the traditional account of morality, as outside of politics. Tronto leaves unanswered, however, the difficult question of whether it is useful to make the distinction between the moral and the political at all, once she challenges the boundary between the two. Given her focus on "getting the work of care done," it is not clear that such an analytical problem is directly relevant.

The challenge Tronto presents is a critical one if we are to take care as a practice seriously, for if we set care outside of practice as a principle to govern it, all the difficult questions about how care is actualized remain unanswered. Yet if we abandon the principle for the political, it is not entirely clear how we would criticize current practices of care. Tronto's explicit concern for the politics of care prompts her consideration of the relationship between ethics and justice. The rules of justice as they are embodied in our institutions become relevant to a practice of care; in particular, they become relevant to the question Who cares for whom? Such a question is clearly critical, given the analysis presented of the cases.

Tronto understands care itself as a practice rather than as either a principle or an emotion. In this sense, she separates herself clearly from Noddings.[4] But she also recognizes that the dominant institutional framework in a liberal political culture like ours is a justice framework. "Getting the work of care done" requires that we recognize this and move on from there. Care is a practice rather than a principle formulated in abstraction from practice, and it is a practice located within the larger context of justice-oriented institutions.

As a practice, care involves both caregiving and care receiving. Tronto locates these roles within a political context, noting that care giving is often undervalued and that much of care receiving goes unacknowledged as such. She explores the practice of care in the context of race, class, and gender dynamics:

4. Bubeck (1995) describes Noddings's work as focused on caring as an attitude rather than as an activity, and the sense of caring that she is concerned with as psychological cum moral. Bubeck herself argues that the attitude of caring and activity of caring most often go together but that the connection is "slightly looser than we might ideally hope for" (see 147–53). But for those like Tronto, who take the political problem of organizing care seriously, the role that institutions play in facilitating appropriate attitudes and activities of caring is critical. In this sense the vision of care as "psychological cum moral" is rejected.

Caring is often constituted socially in a way that makes caring work into the work of the least well off members of society. It is difficult to know whether the least well off are less well off because they care and caring is devalued, or because in order to devalue people they are forced to do caring work. Nevertheless, if we look at questions of race, class and gender, we notice that those who are least well off in society are disproportionately those who do the work of caring, and that the best off members of society often use their positions of superiority to pass caring work off to others. (Tronto 1993, 113)

Tronto does not reduce the distribution of caring to the intentional efforts by those in positions of power to exploit others. Rather, she sees a complex relationship of ideas about individualism, autonomy, and the "self-made" man at work in the distribution of care: "These 'self-made' figures would not only find it difficult to admit the degree to which care has made their lives possible, but such an admission would undermine the legitimacy of the inequitable distribution of power, resources and privilege of which they are beneficiaries" (1993, 111).

The distribution of care, and particularly the place of care in addressing the needs of the privileged, the marginal, and primarily private place of care, preserve a particular social order. When Tronto challenges the boundary between the political and the moral, she opens up the space for care to take its "proper place" and makes legitimate the posing of questions such as Who cares for whom? For once care is denaturalized, located within the political, "the proper place" of care and questions about who cares for whom are open to debate; they cannot be taken for granted. As interviews with the Beacons coordinators illustrated, attentiveness to the identity of those involved in the practices of care was critical both to their critique of the conventional organization of public care and to their reformulation of these practices.

Care and Distributive Justice

Raising such questions about the distribution of care would seem critical to taking the politics of care seriously. Both Tronto and Diemut Bubeck suggest that it is here that justice has a role to play, and they are both, at least in part, reacting to Noddings here.

Diemut Bubeck begins with the question, "When the needs of two people are mutually exclusive, how do we resolve this as carers?" (1995, 201). She observes that making a decision to act here cannot merely depend on having a detailed enough assessment of the needs of both persons. Action can ensue only after one alternative between the two has been chosen as the right, desirable, or just one; and this often involves a calculation about minimizing harm by responding to the greater need. She notes, "The principle of responding to greater need involves a kind of calculus that Noddings denies her carers engage in but involves distributive justice" (206). Conflicting demands on care require justice to resolve them. In this sense, principles of justice must form an organic part of the practice of care.

Yet Bubeck acknowledges that principles must play a different role here than they do in a Kantian or utilitarian model. They do not straightforwardly dictate decisions; they have a less prominent role than in conventional models of justice. They are important, particularly to questions regarding the distribution of care in the public sphere, for here care is subject to the requirements of impartiality. Again, she seems to directly respond to the dilemma presented in Noddings:

> [I]t may be the case that carers need to draw boundaries if they are to prevent their caring disposition from being exploited but there is a further question as to which boundaries are justified. Prejudice and parochialism certainly do not provide justifiable boundaries, nor does their existence prove that the disposition to care itself has boundaries. (1995, 224)

The distribution of care in the public sphere should therefore follow two principles: the harm minimization principle and the principle of equality, in that both principles express and satisfy the requirements of impartiality (235). Harm minimization requires that each person's need is to count for one and nobody's need for more than one, and equality requires that everybody's needs be taken into equal consideration and to some extent be met.

Needs here become commodities for exchange, enabling us to talk about a fair distribution in terms of a market model of exchange where each person's need equals one. But reflection on the case studies suggests that we cannot take for granted a consensus on what counts as needs and that the problem of defining what will count as my one need is a real one. These general rules are, I assume, meant to ensure that each need is met with (one) care. Yet the case studies also suggest that the problem of separating care from the caregiver who is assessing needs, who is doing the work of care, seems to matter very much. The process of commodifying care to ensure fair distribution is premised on our ability to complete this separation.

Moreover, Bubeck herself seems conflicted about the generality of rules governing the allocation of care, and it is unclear exactly how impartiality can be made compatible with care so that distributive models of justice work. This conflict is most evident in her discussion of "relatedness." She understands relatedness as referring to a kind of personalized relationship between people in which individual people who have personal knowledge of each other, who have a shared history between them, and who feel emotionally close and involved with, as well as committed to, each other on the basis of, and because of, their mutual knowledge and shared history (222). It is relatedness in this sense that the case studies revealed as a critical background for getting the work of care done.

Bubeck argues that the difference between care in the public sphere and care in the private sphere is the presence or absence of relatedness as the ground of care. She says that while relatedness may justifiably influence the amount and type of care given, it does not necessarily make a difference to the quality of care (224, 229). While these two claims may be difficult to reconcile, they are motivated by an admirable concern to extend care to strangers, to avoid Noddings's dilemma: "The absence of relatedness, however, does not necessarily imply the absence of any impulse to act on behalf of others who are more or less unknown strangers" (223). She is seeking to address the potential for neglect. The case studies suggest that Bubeck's earlier claim that relatedness influences the process of care is on the mark. But the absence of relatedness also seems relevant to explaining the failures of public care in the New Futures model. While Bubeck's turn to distributive justice is intended to remedy the problem of parochialism, "the unfortunate association of the ethic of care with particularism," it does so by commodifying both needs and care in order to allow us to talk about fair exchange. But if things like relatedness are relevant to care as a process, such a distributive model will often fail to match needs with appropriate care.

Joan Tronto's turn to distributive justice also begins as an attempt to avoid the problems presented by Noddings. She is chiefly concerned to move beyond the model of the family as a model of care. Again, Tronto seems to be speaking directly to Noddings when she writes:

> The only way that transforming the political realm into "one big happy family" can work is to import with that notion some ideas that seem inherent in family life: hierarchy, unity, partiality, that are anathema to a liberal, democratic society. Indeed it was to escape from a familialistic understanding of politics that a modern liberalism was born in the seventeenth century. (1993, 169)

The family as a model for care risks reproducing a distribution of care that Tronto sees as clearly gendered. It also simultaneously locates this gendered care outside of politics. Again, returning to the question Who cares for whom? Tronto wants an attentiveness to relations of power in society, and, she argues, "It requires a hard look at questions of justice, as we determine which needs to meet" (172), and "Obviously a theory of justice is necessary to discern among more and less urgent needs" (138).

By Tronto's account, to answer the question Who should care for whom? seems to require a justice framework. Tronto warns against thinking about needs as "a commodity. Such a commodification or reification of needs obscures the processes of care necessary to meeting needs" (138). Yet she also says that it is obvious that "a theory of justice is necessary to discern among more and less urgent needs" (138). Care seems to have become a good, and justice the means for distributing that good. Distribution becomes an issue because the demand for care may exceed the "supply." This causes many of the same conflicts Noddings had noted in our earlier discussion. Tronto frames the conflict in these terms: "Often caregivers will find that their needs to care for themselves come in conflict with the care that they must give to others, or that they are responsible to take care of a number of other persons or things whose needs are in conflict with one another" (109). This distributive dilemma has obvious consequences for the quality of care.

Whereas Noddings attempted to deal with conflict and distribution within care by distinguishing the inner circle from more distant strangers, Tronto takes recourse to justice in ordering our caring relationships. I have already suggested some of the problems with Noddings's approach. Among other things, by neglecting the issue of how our inner circles come to be bounded as such and treating them as primarily or derivatively natural, she neglects the social and political sources of those boundaries and therefore leaves them unchallenged. Tronto, on the other hand, is clearly aware that caring relationships are not natural but political; "inner circles" reflect and reconstitute relationships of social, political, and economic power. Given such awareness, Tronto is able to take a much more critical perspective in addressing the distribution of care.

But I am not sure that recourse to justice, at least in the manner I read Tronto suggesting, is the answer. First, if care is a practice, how is it that the *practices* of care fit together with the *principles* of justice? Again, we must ask if they are, or if they can be made, compatible. Does it make sense to define care as a practice and then treat it as a good? The distributive principles of justice may not encourage an awareness of factors like identity, negotiation, and responsiveness, which are relevant to the practices of care. But while a justice framework may not encourage such an awareness, it is perhaps arguable that it permits it. Even so, we face the hard question: If care is a good and justice is the principle that governs its distribution, what is there to suggest that justice would not just reallocate care in the manner it has always done, privatizing and devaluing it? The questions Tronto poses about the distribution of care in society seem not to come from within the justice framework, for just distribution has long been equated with market distribution where issues of identity and power are supposed to be irrelevant. If Tronto wants to retain a place for justice in the context of her argument about care, it would seem to require the reconstruction of justice so that it is not so tightly associated with market distribution. And in fact she acknowledges that "the kind of theory of justice that will be necessary to determine needs is probably different from most current theories of justice" (138).

Tronto is concerned that her argument that "care" take its proper political place not be read as an assertion that care is a total account of morality: "[I]t is not meant to overthrow such moral precepts as do not lie, do not break promises, avoid harm to others" (126). I agree with Tronto that "care should not be taken as a total account of morality." Yet the turn to justice to fill out a vision of morality seems problematic. If justice is to govern distribution, care will end up, it would seem, as a good distributed to those who are "needy," and uniquely so in relation to the norm of autonomy and self-sufficiency assumed within a justice orientation. Again, if we maintain the vision of autonomy as self-sufficiency, the need for care implies a deviance from the norm that justifies paternalism. All of these are problems that Tronto recognizes in the justice orientation, and thus, in bringing justice and care together, she understands there to be a necessary modification of the justice framework. However, it is not entirely clear how, in treating it as the framework for distributing care, the justice framework has evolved beyond the original understanding of it that Tronto critiques.

The Politics of Needs Interpretation

At the outset of this chapter I said that I had sympathies with the political impetus behind many of the attempts to bring justice and care together. Here both Joan Tronto and Seyla Benhabib argue that attention to the politics of needs interpretation is critical to recognizing the potential for domination and resisting it.

Tronto acknowledges paternalism and parochialism as two primary dangers of care as a political ideal: "[T]he only solution that I see to these two problems is to insist that care needs to be connected to a theory of justice and to be relentlessly democratic in its disposition" (1993, 171). She focuses specifically on the problem of "needs interpretation"—a process that she says must necessarily involve both care receivers and caregivers: "Only in a democratic process where recipients are taken seriously, rather than being automatically delegitimized because they are needy, can needs be evaluated consistent with an ethic of care" (139).

Yet in order to achieve such a democratic politics, we must move beyond a static vision of the roles of caregivers and caretakers. To Tronto's credit, she takes relationships of power between providers and recipients seriously: "Often care-givers have more competence and expertise in meeting the needs of those receiving care. The result is that care-givers may well come to see themselves as more capable of assessing the needs of care-receivers than are the care-receivers themselves" (1993, 170). But in taking power seriously, one always runs the risk of a depiction of the positions of providers and recipients as fixed: "[A]ll humans have different needs and thus we can say that some people are more needy than others" (172). It is not entirely clear how we went from "different needs" to "more needy," though it is undeniably a belief widely expressed in the context of public policy debate that there are "needy" people. Because needs are "culturally determined," Tronto believes this inequity in needs can be addressed. But it seems a thoroughgoing commitment to an interpretive politics of needs would have to challenge the idea that some are "more needy" than others.

Here again, needs come to sound as though they are properties of individuals. This may become a justification for a rather static division of labor between providers and recipients of care. While we may, as Tronto suggests, evaluate and change the distribution of care, we are unlikely to challenge this division of labor. As the Beacons programs demonstrate, and as I will argue at greater length in my concluding chapter, a commitment to a democratic politics of care requires the recognition that democratic citizens are simultaneously both providers and recipients of care. This recognition challenges the authority of those previously understood as normal and self-sufficient to define the needs of those understood as uniquely (deviantly) not so and suggests the need for explicit attention to the process of interpreting needs.

Seyla Benhabib (1987) has focused her efforts to bring justice and care together on what she calls a "communicative theory of needs interpretation." Does her conceptual framework more adequately recognize the politics involved in the process of needs interpretation? Does it provide remedies to the problem of domination, of providers speaking for others in the course of defining needs?

Benhabib argues that a communicative theory of needs interpretation requires a move away from the Rawlsian original position and more generally from the contractarian vision of the self to a view of the relational self. She is critical of universalistic moral theories in the Western tradition because they are substitutionalist "in the sense that the universalism they defend is defined surreptitiously by identifying the experiences of a specific group of subjects as the paradigmatic case of all humans" (1987, 158). Kohlberg and Rawls illustrate an epistemic incoherence in their universalistic moral theories. She describes this incoherence in the following terms:

> [A]ccording to Kohlberg and Rawls, moral reciprocity involves the capacity to take the standpoint of the other, to put oneself imaginatively in the place of the other, but under conditions of the "veil of ignorance," the other as different from the self disappears. . . . Differences are not denied, they become irrelevant. (165)

Rawls's veil of ignorance assumes that those behind the veil are transcendental selves, selves "epistemologically and metaphysically prior to individual characteristics" (166). Benhabib argues that this problematizes Rawls's commitment to universality:

If, therefore, there is no human *plurality* behind the veil of ignorance but only *definitional identity* then this has consequences for
criteria of reversibility and universalizability, said to be a constitu-
ent of the moral point of view. Definitional identity leads to *incomplete reversibility*, for the primary requisite of reversibility, namely,
a coherent distinction between me and you, the self and the other,
cannot be sustained under these circumstances. Under conditions of
the veil of ignorance, the other disappears. (166)

Benhabib's sensitivity to the dilemmas of identity, to the problem of sub-
stitutionalism, seems to speak directly to the analysis of the case studies. In
attempting to develop a conceptual framework sensitive to difference, Benhabib does not reject the aspiration to universalism altogether. She distinguishes what she calls "substitutionalist" from "interactive" universalism:
"Interactive universalism acknowledges the plurality of modes of being human, and differences among humans, without endorsing all these plu-
ralities and differences as morally and politically valid" (158). In several
senses, the impetus for the move away from the substitutionalist to the
interactive form of universalism parallels moves associated with Gilligan's
"care": both Gilligan and Benhabib begin by taking "embodied and embedded identity" as a starting point. In labeling this form of universalism
interactive rather than substitutionalist, Benhabib marks her concern to
avoid both domination and neglect and her unwillingness to give up concepts like fairness, reciprocity, and some universalizable procedure as ways
of judging what will be considered morally and politically valid. This requires some sense of the generalized other:

[W]e abstract from the individuality and concrete identity of the
other. We assume that the other, like ourselves, is a being with concrete needs, desires and affects, but what constitutes moral dignity
is not what differentiates us from each other, but rather what we, as
speaking and acting rational agents, have in common. Our relation
to the other is governed by the norms of *formal equality* and *reciprocity*: each is entitled to expect and assume from us what we can
expect and assume from him or her. (163)

Yet Benhabib also wants to reject the claim that such a vision of the "generalized other" requires that difference "disappear."
Benhabib places the concrete and the generalized other in relation to one

another by rejecting starting points such as the social contract position (which she says denies difference) and the "veil of ignorance" (where difference "disappears") and replacing them with a communicative ethic of needs interpretation. This communicative ethic begins not with hypothetical but with actual dialogues between "moral agents." The deliberation is not limited by epistemic constraints on moral reasoning—the more knowledge of actual situations, "the more rational will be the outcome of their deliberations" (169). And because there are no epistemic constraints, Benhabib argues, it follows that there is no privileged subject matter. Finally, communicative ethics of needs interpretation may challenge the very conditions and constraints under which such dialogues occur. There are no rules of deliberation, of the bargaining game, that must be accepted prior to the choice of principles of justice. "A consequence of this model of communicative ethics would be that the language of rights and duties can now be challenged in light of our need interpretations" (170). Benhabib's concept of interactive universalism is helpful in some important ways. It seems to suggest that general rules fairly applied can be derived from actual selves rather than requiring abstract selves. This provides room for a more comprehensive conception of fairness, one that does not have to bracket concrete differences associated with our nonpublic selves: "[O]ur affective emotional constitution, as well as our concrete history as moral agents, ought to be considered accessible to moral communication, reflection, and transformation" (170). Yet her work also demonstrates the difficulties of assuming too close a relationship between an epistemological shift and a political shift. As an alternative to the original position, the communicative ethic of needs interpretation is supposed to be "emancipatory." But this raises several concerns mentioned earlier. First, as with voice, communication involves more than an expressive component. It must, particularly if it is to be emancipatory, involve a responsive component. In situating moral agents in dialogue with one another, what is it about the relationship that makes dialogue productive? Put another way, is there any reason, given that actual moral subjects take their embedded, embodied selves to the dialogue, to believe that those privileged prior to the dialogue will not reproduce their privilege within it? Even if there are not "privileged subject matters," might there be privileged subjects? Benhabib's model admits difference and plurality to the dialogue but seems to assume we can bracket the relationships of power that are often the sources of those differences. Second, this bracketing seems to enable Benhabib to assume that the outcome of this communicative process of needs interpretation is a complementary relationship across differences. Benhabib's vision of the concrete other that we abstract from to constitute our commonality recognizes that "[o]ur differences in this case complement rather than exclude one another" (170). She writes, "[T]he self only becomes an 'I' in a community of other selves who are also 'I's.' Every act of self-reference expresses simultaneously the uniqueness and difference of the self as well as the commonality among selves" (170). This commonality makes possible "complementarity" among selves.

The vision of the relational self may be helpful in rejecting the contractarian version of the self, but I am not sure it accomplishes the conceptual complementarity Benhabib suggests. In locating the concrete *I* as a product of socialization, Benhabib seems to assume a compatibility of *I*'s that is perhaps morally (given her vision of moral), but not politically, tenable. If the *I* becomes an *I* in a community of selves, relationships seem not merely to be contingent to the self but constitutive of the self. And many of these relationships are embedded in dynamics of inequality and domination. To bracket the power associated with these dynamics is to neglect a primary part of the identity of these actual selves.

Can such an "anticipatory-utopian" critique of needs interpretation serve as a guide, a regulative ideal, for practice? "The point is not to juxtapose the generalized to the concrete other or to seek normative validity in one or another standpoint. The point is to think through the ideological limitations and biases that arise in the discourse of universalist morality through this unexamined opposition" (169). Despite her emphasis on "actual moral agents," Benhabib's version of a merger between Kohlberg and Gilligan focuses on how we think about the problems of justice and care, and the connection between this and actually "getting the work of care done" remains relatively unarticulated. And there are ways in which this step away from the difficult questions of practice limit the utility of her framework for practice. Benhabib's move to take seriously needs interpretation, while recognizing that needs are both cause and consequence of historical social relations, is critical. But what seems inadequately attended to are the relationships of power and domination that stabilize this history. It seems difficult to imagine that actual rather than hypothetical moral agents, in light of these actual relationships, would be able to produce a complementary vision of their difference. Here the commitment to formal equality and reciprocity embodied in the generalized other must govern interactive relations, again bracketing power. Benhabib offers a "communicative ethic of needs interpretation" that does not seem to address the problems of a political process of needs interpretation.

The contrast between Tronto and Benhabib is instructive, for in focusing on "getting the work of care done," Tronto takes the problems of political practice seriously and is attentive to the relationships of political power that are the background against which we organize the process of care. But in taking the power of providers seriously, there is the risk of leaving their position unchallenged when we reorganize care in an attempt to democratize it. By contrast, Benhabib seems to offer a challenge to our current thinking about care, yet despite beginning with "actual moral agents," the compatibility produced by a communicative ethic requires that we leave much of our actuality behind, specifically our positions with respect to the organization of political power. Left behind, political power goes inadequately recognized in current practices and ultimately inadequately remedied in their alternative. How do we both recognize and realistically challenge the relationships of power that surround care?

Conclusion: Justice, Care, and Democracy

I began by suggesting, in light of both my own work and case studies by others, that there seemed to be a political impetus for raising questions about the relationship between care and justice. In particular, I raised the question of whether it makes sense to ask, Is caring ever unjust? And if so, how do we use a justice orientation to remedy care? I read Gilligan as ambivalent on the question of the relationship between justice and care. Both Tronto and Gilligan attempt to bring care and justice together while also offering arguments that these frameworks as they are currently conceived are based in fundamentally incompatible assumptions. And Bubeck remarks, "[T]he scope of any ethic of care is limited and care is therefore in need of (some) complementary considerations of justice which it cannot generate by itself and which, indeed, are incompatible with its very foundations" (1995, 249). Given the political impetus for raising questions of whether care is "unjust," given a concern to avoid both in order to avoid domination and neglect, is there a political if not theoretical necessity to reconceptualize the relationship between the two? Noddings's reply seems to be no. She argues for a version of care that she claims is capable of guiding all decisions about care. I suggested that because she views care as either primarily or derivatively a product of affective ties, controversial questions like Who should care for whom? and Who gets included in caring? get inadequate treatment in her work. While Noddings helpfully recognizes the role of affect in social relations, she treats affect as natural in a sense outside of politics and therefore not subject to change by a reordering of politics. Ironically, her work on care might defend neglect — neglect of those outside the parochial community.

In this sense, Tronto's work is much more amenable to political discussion. Political concerns with care seem to revolve around the two key dilemmas Tronto pointed to — paternalism and parochialism. Both seem to require a focus on the prior question, Who cares for whom? In the case of paternalism, we might worry if this question assumes a relatively permanent relationship of dependence, rather than mutual respect in the context of recognized interdependence. In the case of parochialism, we might worry if those who have the resources to care consistently focus their caring attention on a select few, severely neglecting others. But unlike Noddings, who seems to take maternalism and parochialism for granted as natural, seeing these phenomena as cause and consequence of politics, Tronto can turn to politics to reorder these relationships.

Tronto, Bubeck, and Benhabib attempt to bring justice and care together to address inadequacies they see in the care framework. Benhabib, however, focuses on the epistemological inadequacies of the justice framework, and her "anticipatory-utopian" vision of an alternative never seems to get beyond that. Dialogue, despite the fact that it is supposed to be "actual" and not "hypothetical," is supposed to result in a complementarity of differences. But in the context of actual issues of power and domination, I fear that such an epistemological complementarity refuses or neglects the possibility of fundamentally conflicting political interests. Tronto's work locates care in relation to a political critique of justice and thus manages to advance care as a political response.

Yet in bringing justice and care together, most work is inadequate in developing the actual fit of the two. In some important ways justice, as we now think of it, and care are based in conflicting assumptions about the self and the social relations that derive from the self. The turn to distributive justice as a guide to allocating care reveals some of these incompatibilities, for to treat care as a good rather than as a process is to miss the relational aspect of care. Furthermore, as Noddings and Benhabib demonstrate, the move to a relational self does not necessarily imply a move to the political self; that is, it is possible to talk about a socially situated self without acknowledging domination as relevant. A democratic politics of care would require the recognition of care as a process and remedies for domination as it occurs in this process. It is not clear that the turn to justice as it has thus far been formulated can provide fairness as a remedy without simultaneously commodifying care.

5

Does Justice Require Care?

The Problem of Empathy and Knowing

The last chapter reviewed work that attempted to supplement "care" with "justice." Having examined the practices of public care, I argued that these practices, situated within the conventional institutional context, were often inadequate to meeting the needs of recipients. In light of this I asked, "Is the incorporation of justice into a care framework necessary to remedy these shortcomings?" Reviewing the work of Gilligan, Noddings, Tronto, and Benhabib with this in mind, I concluded that much of this literature is helpful in illustrating the inadequacies of care frameworks that take care to be a comprehensive guide to moral and political decision making. However, I also suggested that the attempts to supplement care with justice in order to avoid these inadequacies often failed to produce either coherent conceptual alternatives or adequate guides to practice.

This chapter addresses two alternative accounts of the relationship between justice and care. These accounts, however, differ in nature from those discussed in the previous chapter. Rather than arguing that care might require justice as a supplement to provide a more adequate account of morality, Susan Okin and Robert Solomon have argued that, in fact, care has always had a place within the dominant frameworks for thinking about justice. Thus, rather than framing the question as Card does: Might care require justice to avoid evil? or as Tronto and Bubeck do: Might care require justice to handle distributive conflicts? or as Gilligan does: Might care require justice for the incorporation of the self? Okin and Solomon begin by asking how care might already be an inadequately acknowledged component of our theories of justice. Their concern is that the way we often tell the story of justice simultaneously relies on and requires care but also neglects its explicit consideration. Both Okin and Solomon argue that some element of care, compassion, or empathy is necessary to make sense of social contract theory as well as the practices that follow from it. Thus, by comparison with the work in the previous chapter that sought a kind of complementary balance between justice and care, Okin and Solomon begin by presuming that justice and care, properly conceptualized, are not com-plementary alternatives to one another, but rather are integral components of a politics committed to fairness.

In each of their respective works, Okin and Solomon begin by challeng-ing the dichotomy assumed by the "care versus justice" formulation, and they do so in similar ways. Okin's "Reason and Feeling in Thinking About Justice" (1990) and Solomon's *A Passion for Justice* (1990) challenge the dualisms that pair care with emotion and justice with reason. Both argue that the contractarian vision requires, albeit implicitly, a certain associa-tion with the emotions in order to be coherent. Okin focuses on the role of empathy in Rawls's work; Solomon suggests the place of emotion in the context of a much longer history of contractarian thought. Ultimately, while Okin — rightly, I think — argues that empathy is an inadequately at-tended to aspect of Rawls's work, I will argue that Rawls's use of empathy fails to bring together care and justice in a manner that can remedy the concerns raised in the case studies. The focus of my critique here is the claim made by both Rawls and Okin that the commitment to empathy is compatible with impartiality. But I am not merely concerned with the con-ceptual difficulty that this claim poses. I also want to argue that empathy, so conceived, is unable to respond to many of the critiques of a justice framework launched by advocates of care. Specifically, an understanding of care and the empathetic sense from which it is derived as a contextual and particular response to needs seems inconsistent with the notion of empathy as Rawls and Okin conceptualize it.[1] Such a vision of empathy as impartiality, as we will see in greater detail in the following chapter, can be invoked to defend paternalistic relationships of authority in which empathy becomes a way of knowing what others need without engaging them as particular others.

Solomon also challenges the strict division between emotion and reason that contractarian thought seems to require. But he offers a close consideration of the relationship between care, emotion, and context, suggesting that it is the particularistic nature of emotion—that is, its "context specificness"—that threatened contractarian understandings of political rationality and that ultimately explains the neglect of explicit consideration of emotion in contractarian thought. In formulating the problem of the reason/emotion dualism in this way, Solomon refuses the reducibility of empathy to the dominant model of rationality. Whereas in the Rawls/Okin formulation empathy becomes a way of knowing that mirrors traditional liberal/positivist epistemologies, Solomon rejects a model of knowing that subordinates emotion to reason and instead suggests emotion in the form of compassion as an alternative way of knowing, necessarily experientially linked.

The distinction here is critical. There are markedly different political consequences of construing empathy as a way of knowing where conventional models of epistemology are left unchallenged, and of construing it as a way of relating. Rawls and Okin seem to treat empathy as a device or vehicle for gaining knowledge, the content of which is not fundamentally different from the knowledge gained through a rational consideration traditionally conceived. In this sense, Okin's argument that empathy is necessary to justice does not imply a challenge to traditional practices of care. By contrast, Solomon's critique of contractarian rationality leads him to conceptualize knowing itself in a manner that implies a challenge to liberal epistemology. He effectively resists the common temptation to value the particular only in light of what it might contribute to one's ability to make universalizable claims.

This version of knowing, as Solomon lays it out, gives the emotions a place in both perception and judgment. And Solomon allies himself with

1. I have suggested that while Gilligan defines the care orientation as contextual and differentiates it from Kohlberg's framework for moral reasoning in exactly this way, Noddings's understanding of need essentializes need, and thus her work on care relies on a conception of empathy that may be compatible with that of Rawls and Okin.

Lawrence Blum in suggesting that "because compassion involves an active and objective interest in another's interest, it is characteristically a spur to deeper understanding than rationality alone could ensure. A person who is compassionate by character is in principle committed to as rational and as intelligent a course of action as possible" (1990, 234). Ultimately this re-constructed version of knowing protects particularity and, as I will argue in the final section of this chapter, offers one element of a defense of the critical participation necessary for a democratic politics of care.

Okin on Reason, Feeling, and Rawls

Okin begins her defense of Rawlsian justice by arguing that "some recent distinctions that have been made between an ethic of justice and an ethic of care, may be at least overdrawn, if not false" (1990, 15). While Okin acknowledges that the influence of Kant on Rawls leads to the expression of his major ideas in the language of rational choice, she argues that this language leaves Rawls unnecessarily open to criticism: "Whereas Rawls's theory is sometimes viewed as excessively rationalistic, individualistic and abstracted from real human beings, I will argue that, at its center (though frequently obscured by Rawls himself) is a voice of responsibility, care and concern for others" (1990, 16). As an example, Okin suggests Rawls's focus on the family as a critical institution for socialization, presumably of socialization to caring. Okin does criticize Rawls for uncritically accepting the family in its conventional patriarchal form. Her critique is that Rawls neglects the issue of the justice or injustice of the gendered family itself. But she argues that his attention to the family as a site critical to continued moral development marks Rawls as having a fundamentally more ade-quate account of moral development than he is often given credit for. She argues that Rawls sees the family as necessary to teaching us the impor-tance of thinking through moral dilemmas from the role perspective of others: "Participation in different roles in the various associations of soci-ety leads to the development of a person's 'capacity for fellow feeling' and to 'ties of friendship and mutual trust.' "[2]

Okin draws out this part of Rawls in order to illustrate a distinction between Rawls and Kant that has significance for the role of mutual trust.

2. Rawls 1971, 470, quoted in Okin 1990, 22.

She argues that Rawls sees the capacity for fellow feeling as derivative of experience and valuable as such. By contrast, Kant, she says, viewed any feelings that did not follow from independently established moral principles as morally suspect. While I think Okin's work is helpful in demonstrating an important difference between some aspects of the work of Rawls and that of Kant, I would raise two critical questions. First, How does this distinction work, given certain crucial similarities between Rawls and Kant, particularly their commitment to an original position outside of experience from which political arrangements are derived? Second, Can Rawls maintain his end of this distinction and still defend his version of the original position?

Okin seems to read Rawls as suggesting an original position in which experience (for example, the experience of growing up in a family) contributes both to the capacity to know (via fellow feeling) and to the content of knowledge. There are, she says, no limits on the general information available. Yet simultaneously, those in the original position deliberate to determine political arrangements from behind a "veil of ignorance." Taken together, these seem to require contradictory depictions of the contractee. Rawls wants his "veil" to ensure that thinking through justice is not influenced by one's class position, social status, or personal attributes. Okin reads Rawls here as making a virtue of self-interest in the sense that the veil converts what would, without its presence, be self-interest, into equal concern for others. Those behind the veil must think from the position of everybody. And having been socialized in small associations such as the family, they are prepared to do so.

Okin is willing to acknowledge that there are certain aspects of Rawls's work that sound committed to rational choice. But this, she says, is misleading. In fact, she argues, Rawls brings together both a commitment to universal principles of justice and a recognition of the importance of empathy to their realization:

> If we, who *do* know who we are, are to think *as if* we were in the original position, we must develop considerable capacities for empathy and powers of communication with others about what different human lives are like. But these alone are not enough to maintain in us a sense of justice. Since we know who we are and what are our particular interests and conceptions of the good, we need as well a great commitment to benevolence; to caring about each and every other as much as about ourselves. (1990, 32)

I find both Rawls and Okin confusing on this point, and I am not yet persuaded by attempts to suggest that care has such a functional place within justice. If Okin has Rawls right, both want to say that the original position is a theoretical, in the sense of hypothetical, approach to deriving the principles of justice — that it requires both capacities dependent on particular concrete experiences (experiences within the family or associations that produce a sense of identification or membership, for example) and simultaneously requires that the actual content of those experiences be left behind. Yet if experience can be so easily reformulated into a distinction between the *content* of experience and the *capacity* to experience, it is not clear how this differs from the capacity to theorize, as it has traditionally been conceived. How is this capacity different from the capacity to think rationally through moral dilemmas in the way rational choice models assume? Put another way, the attachment to experience — at least as feminist theorists such as Lorraine Code and Alison Jaggar, and pragmatists such as Cornel West and, of course, John Dewey understand it — has largely been an attachment to the idea that the capacities of a subject and subjectivity itself are not easily separated. The vision of subjectivity that assumes such an easy split is uniquely the product of what I called in Chapter 1 "a modern understanding of the self." Thomas Spragens (1981) depicts the self of modernity as one whose attachment to autonomous reason requires a commitment to scientific method that makes the particular subjectivity of the knower irrelevant. What Gilligan calls "the caring self" poses a fundamental challenge to this version of rational man exactly because it retrieves and legitimizes "particularity."[3] But in Okin's interpretation of Rawls, empathy loses this association with particularity.

The recognition of the inseparability of principle (or the capacity for principled thought) from the context in which principle was applied was a critical distinguishing feature of the care orientation Gilligan identified and contrasted with Kohlberg's Kantian version of justice. She understood her challenge to traditional conceptions of moral development as in part giving experience its proper place in the resolution of moral dilemmas. Experi-

---

3. Meredith Michaels (1986) suggests that Gilligan herself is not entirely consistent on this point. She argues that Gilligan's distinction between psychological and formal reason is actually based in a relationship of mutual interdependence: "At the very least, particular applications of justice principles presuppose a desire to act justly, and it is difficult to see how that desire could spring up independently of an agent's psychology. . . . To the extent that in appealing to an ethic of care, a person engages in reasoning, she is employing formal logic" (182).

ence refuses any easy separation between capacity, on the one hand, and the *use* of capacity, which requires context, on the other hand. In this sense, experience is necessarily relational. Gilligan notes that the commitment to the centrality of experience requires an epistemological shift: "The moral domain's underlying epistemology shifts from the Greek ideal of knowledge as a correspondence between mind and form to the biblical conception of knowing as a process of human relationships" (1993, 173). While her description of this epistemological position as a "biblical conception" is not particularly helpful, it is clear that Gilligan has a relational model of knowing in mind.

Moreover, I am not sure what empathy would look like as a capacity for fellow feeling, without a particular object, or for that matter a particular subject (that is, a subject with features such as gender, race, and religious orientation).[4] Okin writes:

> It is certainly the case that Rawls's construction of the original position is designed so as to eliminate from the formulation of the principles of justice biases that might result from particular attachments to others as well as from particular facts about the self. Surely impartiality in this sense is a reasonable requirement to make a theory of justice. But nevertheless, as I have argued here, the only coherent way in which a party thinks through justice is through empathy with persons . . . especially the least well off in various respects. To think as a person in the original position is not to be a disembodied nobody. . . . Rather it is to think from the perspective of everybody, of every "concrete other" whom one might turn out to be. (1990, 34)

Okin seems here again to be moving back and forth between suggesting that Rawls "requires real motivations on the part of real human beings" and that this (personal motivations) is exactly what is left behind in the original position.

Furthermore, there appears to be a basis for both accounts of Rawls in the original text. Rawls writes, "To be sure, any principles chosen in the original position may require a large sacrifice for some. The beneficiaries of clearly unjust institutions may find it hard to reconcile themselves to the

---

4. Here I think we are revisiting Benhabib's concern about incomplete reversibility behind the veil of ignorance in a different form.

changes that will have to be made."[5] Yet by Rawls's earlier account, this seems to give too much credit to those here understood as motivated to sacrifice; for it is exactly his earlier point that the original position is a situation in which we would be ignorant of our own position and thus unable to discern ourselves as sacrificing or benefiting. Of course, it might be possible for Rawls to claim that the motivation for the formulation of principles such as his difference principle is not self-sacrifice or benevolence, but rather justice itself. However, if his claim is, as Okin contends, that the motivation of sacrifice or benevolence is relevant to producing justice — and in her view this is the way in which care already has its place within justice — then we have to rethink things. For instance, if I am one who will have to sacrifice, and I take enough knowledge of my own situation to the original position to know that, I may also bring a conception of the good that legitimates my privilege. Reaching consensus on principles of justice would be more difficult once those in the original position are conceded to have some particular identity. Consensus on principles of justice has conventionally been assumed possible exactly because such principles were derived abstracted from such particularities.

Again, Rawls is contradictory on this point. He does want those behind the veil of ignorance to be particular people, but it is not clear how much of one's identity is left behind the veil of ignorance. However, for Okin to claim that benevolence or empathy plays a role, she seems to need certain particularities — one's position of relative privilege, for example — to be available to those behind the veil. After all, the difference principle can only be said to be motivated by benevolence (rather than the rationally calculated self-interest of non-risk-takers) if its proponent is privileged, knows this, and so would be giving rather than getting according to this principle. Or alternatively, the difference principle may be the inevitable consequence of rational thinking about justice — as Rawls clearly suggests at points. But if this is the case, then benevolence and empathy seem to be left behind again, and this threatens Okin's claim that care has a necessary place in Rawls's theory.

Okin sees Rawls as bringing justice and care together in claiming that *both* empathy and impartiality are needed if the original position is to produce appropriate principles of justice. Yet in order for empathy to be made compatible with impartiality, it must be fundamentally redefined in relation to its association with care. Empathy no longer seems to require

5. Quoted in Okin 1990, 17.

relationality. Some of the literature in the field of psychology draws a distinction between empathy as a way of knowing and sympathy as a way of relating.[6] This distinction has gone largely unnoted in the literature on care, yet it seems a significant distinction for organizing work on care and for the way we think about needs. I will return to this point in the concluding section of this chapter. Here I want only to suggest that the term *empathy* is used in several senses, and that empathy as a way of knowing may not be compatible with empathy as a way of relating if knowing is taken to be modeled on conventional liberal/positivist understandings of knowledge. I would argue that this redefinition collapses empathy into traditional models of knowing as abstraction from experience rather than connection to or engagement with it. In this form, it is not clear that empathy or care maintains any of their original association with context. Rawls's version of the original position seems both to require some knowledge of the social content and capacities of selves and to need impartiality achieved through the forgetting of such social content. These seem to be contradictory requirements.

In the next section we will examine Robert Solomon's alternative account of the relationship between justice and care in which care is more adequately associated with compassion, which is necessarily partial, than with empathy as impartiality. Solomon's version of the relationship between justice and care does not subordinate care to the impartiality of justice, but rather grants his understanding of compassion status as a kind of alternative way of knowing. Solomon argues for a legitimate place for partiality in moral decision making, thereby allowing compassion to maintain its autonomy as a species of judgment.

A "Passion" for Justice

In his work entitled *A Passion for Justice,* Robert Solomon uses a consideration of social contract theory to develop a long-standing theme in his work on the relationship between rationality and the emotions. The central contention of his work is that our sense of justice is exactly that—a "sense"—and that therefore justice must first consist in feelings (1990,

---

6. See especially Wispe 1986. Also helpful are Berger 1984, Deutsch and Madle 1975, and Shapiro 1974.

35). What Solomon means by "first" is not that emotions/feelings/senses (as opposed to rationality) are primary, but rather that inclination, feelings, or senses are not separable from obligations in the way that much of our thinking about justice seems to assume:

> It is, to begin with, a dubious distinction — between inclinations and obligations, between our natural existence and our social existence, between the natural disposition of our feelings and the rationality that allows us to form society and then live in it. But it is a vicious dichotomy, emotion versus reason, and these two classic metaphors — "the state of nature" and "the social contract" — have a dangerous appeal for us. They make us distance ourselves from our emotions (falsely conceived of as "natural" and pre-social) and encourage us to entertain the appealing fiction that we live in a society by voluntary choice rather than just because we happened to be born and raised here. (1990, 32–33)

When Solomon writes that his aim is to reintroduce those "lost but essential ingredients of justice" (1990, 202), he may sound like he is making a move similar to Okin's. But while both challenge the assumed dichotomy between care and justice, the source of Solomon's resistance to this opposition is actually quite at odds with Okin's argument. In order to illustrate the distinction and ultimately its political consequences, it is helpful to think through the responses each theorist would offer to the following questions. First, What is the relationship between emotion/care, rationality/justice, and judgment? And second, What is the relationship between emotion/care, and particularity and context?

Okin's response to these two questions centers on her understanding of care and the empathy associated with it as compatible with impartiality. Okin breaks down the care-versus-justice framework by discarding the association of care with context and partiality. She explicitly challenges that association when she writes that "many of the respondents whom Gilligan identifies as speaking in the 'different voice' use it to *express as fully universalizable a morality of social concern* as respondents who express themselves in the language of justice and rights. Thus, the implication frequently drawn from her work, that women's morality tends to be more particularistic and contextual, appears to be unfounded" (1990, 33, emphasis mine).

Leaving aside for the moment the question of whether Okin has Gilligan and her respondents right here, it is clear that Okin wants to resist the move toward contextuality, which she associates with care. She differentiates her own work from other feminist criticisms of Rawls in the following terms:

> While the feminist interpretation of Rawls that I have presented above argues that feelings such as caring and concern for others are essential to the formulation of principles of justice, it does not suggest that such principles can be replaced by contextual caring thinking. The problem, I suggest, is not principles, rules per se, but the ways in which they have been arrived at. If principles of justice are founded, as I have suggested Rawls' are, not on mutual disinterest and detachment from others but on empathy and concern for others—including concern for the way in which others are different from ourselves—they will not be likely to lead to destructive rules. (1990, 33)

Again, "the way principles are arrived at" in Okin's thinking is empathetically; however, our empathetic concern is apparently also impartial. This prevents justice from being "reduced to" merely contextual claims about care.

Empathy and Epistemology

Empathy becomes a way of knowing that is compatible with traditional models of epistemology. As Lorraine Code has noted, these models of epistemology are premised on the assumption that one can substitute any knower for any other knower. Likewise, they take as their starting point the assumption that in the formulation "S knows that p," who S is, is irrelevant to knowing p, and therefore not worthy of attention (1993, 15–16). This formulation of liberal/positivist epistemology suggests why impartiality is critical to Okin's account of justice, for justice consists in knowing, rather than sensing, the proper ordering of social relationships. Emotions here are viewed as obstacles to objectively—that is, impartially—ordering relationships in either the physical or social world. It may be that the reason/emotion split—the positivist understanding of objectivity—is so conventionally embedded that we cannot easily conceptualize an alternative model of knowing. It is the unity of this model of knowing, the way in which moral knowing seems to map onto scientific knowing, that made for its appeal:

> As the Enlightenment saw it, the revolution in knowledge would encompass knowledge of the "ought" as well as of the "is." It would guarantee that men who appropriated the new method would be able to know with unprecedented clarity what they should do as well as what was the case. Knowledge was a unity; moral knowledge was thus to be attainable with the same certainty, clarity, and distinctiveness, the same firm foundations and simplicity as the rest. (Spragens 1981, 61)

Such an epistemological approach is evidenced in the approach taken by Rawls and Okin that weds itself to a veil of ignorance designed to replicate conditions of the neutral scientific observer. Yet as I noted earlier, at least in Gilligan's version of care, she explicitly acknowledges that the care orientation requires an epistemological shift away from this Enlightenment model of knowing.

Code outlines an alternative model of epistemology suggesting the need "to pay as much attention to the nature and situation—the location of S as they [epistemologists] commonly pay to the content of P." A constructivist reorientation, she continues, "requires epistemologists to take subjective factors—factors that pertain to the circumstances of the subject, S— centrally into account in evaluative and justifactory procedures" (1993, 20). Such a model of knowing requires that the particularity of the subject not only have a place but be a focus in a way that Okin's model prohibits. Robert Solomon's work, by contrast, seems compatible with Code's alternative epistemology.

Solomon takes quite a different tack than Rawls and Okin. He is similarly concerned with the way principles are derived. But as his comments suggest, he is concerned about the "dangerous appeal" of concepts like impartiality—concepts he understands as unhelpful theoretical abstractions that are practical impossibilities. The emotions, and care in particular, are not viewed as preventable intrusions that we can shut out by inclining ourselves toward impartiality. To understand justice as requiring impartiality is, in Solomon's view, to misunderstand justice. For justice is not "mere theories," nor is it "an abstract set of principles to be formulated, mastered and imposed upon society" (1990, 45 and 33). "Without care and compassion," he says repeatedly, "there can be no justice" (14). Justice is not opposed to sympathy, it presupposes it.

It may be helpful to begin by articulating exactly what Solomon means by an *emotion*. Solomon argues that what we feel about other people, events, and things generally indicates how we value them: "Emotions are or resemble unspoken value judgments or beliefs" (Calhoun and Solomon, 1984, 16). Emotions, in this sense, perform a rational, evaluative function. This is significant, for in understanding emotion in this way, emotion, care, compassion, and jealousy as well, do not contaminate perception or judgment but rather are essential to it. But perhaps more important for the contrast with Okin, Solomon specifically questions the utility of empathy to care for the following reasons:

> Compassion is a more specific emotion than care . . . related to sympathy or pity. Empathy, we should note, is not so much an emotion of this class as [it is] a technique or strategy for sharing and understanding emotions, an effort to put oneself in the place of another. The most obvious specifying feature of compassion ("suffering with") is that the object of one's concern is somehow in pain. . . . It is often suggested that in compassion one suffers with the other, but one need not actually feel his or her pain oneself. (1990, 225)

Care is understood as "the most general of all emotions. In a broad sense, to have any emotion already presupposes that one cares, that one is engaged, that one has interest, that one, 'takes something personally'" (225).

It is possible to see, by contrasting Solomon's understanding of care with his understanding of empathy, why compassion rather than empathy becomes critical to justice. Solomon acknowledges that as with sympathy, in discussions of compassion there is considerable concern over the idea of a shared emotion. But he makes several moves that I think clarify what is entailed in such sharing. First, part of what Solomon is rejecting in moving to compassion over empathy is the idea that a technique or strategy devoid of any particular content can have utility for care. This is what I referred to earlier as Okin's focus on capacities, say for empathy, without an object. There is nothing about empathy that positions, or in Code's terms "locates," the subject, so it readily gives itself over to the traditional formulation of knowing in which the subject is made irrelevant.

By contrast, compassion is defined as "suffering with" rather than "putting oneself in the other's place." Moreover, compassion defines the location of the subject: "[I]n compassion one suffers with the other, but one need not actually feel his or her pain for oneself; indeed compassion suggests that one somehow stands safely above the misery of the other" (1990, 225). The critical contribution of Solomon's turn to compassion is that it resists the dissolution of feeling or sentiment into something internal to the subject and so maintains compassion as a relation. "It makes good sense but it can be deeply misleading to say that compassion, pity and sympathy are 'feelings,'" he writes. "They are indeed aspects of consciousness . . . but they are also engagements in the world, instances of involving if not identifying oneself with the circumstances and sufferings of other beings" (225).

By understanding emotion, not as an internal state, but rather as an evaluative judgment, Solomon retains a vision of emotion as relational, as having an object outside the self with which the self is engaged. He says, "[V]irtually everything we care about engages rather than abandons the self" (1990, 227). Here we can see the contrast with Rawls/Okin very clearly—for the veil is exactly about abandoning many aspects of the self. This is the crux of Benhabib's critique of substitutionalist universalism. The self behind the veil is epistemologically and metaphysically prior to their individuating characteristics. A model of care based in empathy, where empathy is understood as the displacement of the self and its needs for those of the other, requires just such abandonment. Sarah Hoagland discusses this tendency to self-abandonment in the following terms:

> Certainly relation is central to ethics. However, there must be two beings at least to relate. Moving away from oneself is one aspect of dynamic caring, but it cannot be the only defining element. Otherwise relationship is not ontologically basic, the other is ontologically basic and the self ceases to exist in its own ethical right. There is, as yet, no real relation. (1990, 110–11)

By working from a vision of emotion as essentially about the world, as a way of seeing and engaging the world, rather than as an internal attribute of the self, and by situating both care and justice as requiring engagement with actual others, Solomon is able to maintain the relation as "ontologically basic." He thereby avoids the problem of substitutionalist universalism to which Benhabib refers. He can admit the plurality of perspectives associated with our concrete identities. Thus, to return to Code's epistemological alternative, here we can pay attention to the nature and situation of S and of S's subjectivity, because S has a relational location. S has not been reduced to a definitional identity abstracted from any particular location. This lays the groundwork for taking Code's epistemological shift seriously.

How, then, would Solomon respond to the question posed earlier: What is the relationship between emotion/care, rationality/justice, and judgment? Emotions are a species of judgment, as he understands them: "[O]ur ethics is in part an ethics of emotion (resentment is nasty, love is beautiful); there are right and wrong emotions, and emotion can be right or wrong depending on context and condition" (1990, 53). The emotions are not then viewed as irrational; nor, ironically, is reason as such rational. Rather, both require context and condition; both emotion and reason have meaning only as species of judgment—that is, only as practices of judgment. Neither can be properly or meaningfully understood prior to the act of judgment, for it is judgment that brings them into play with context and establishes their significance as a guide for action.

Thus, where Okin and Solomon begin by questioning the dichotomy between care and justice, Solomon is not satisfied to collapse care into justice as Okin does by assuming that empathy and impartiality are compatible and making impartiality critical to deriving justice. Instead, he says that we must rethink the nature of the distinction. Both emotion and reason, he contends, are species of judgment embedded in, and made sense of, only in particular contexts and sets of conditions. Whereas Okin would answer the question, What is the relationship between emotion/care and context? by suggesting that care is a universalizable guide to moral decision making that can be made compatible with traditional understandings of justice as impartiality, Solomon, it seems, would respond that both emotion and care have meaning only in particular contexts. And upon reflection, the same can be said of justice.

Political Implications: Paternalism and Particularity

Solomon is certainly not alone in his concern about an ethic of care based in empathy. As we saw in the last chapter, Tronto's concern was that empathy might not produce action—that is, getting the work of care done. But there are others who have noted that the consequences of empathy may be potentially more dangerous than sins of omission. Claudia Card notes, for example, that we can take up the perspective of others for some very self-serving reasons; or, alternatively, we may have to take up the perspectives of others merely to survive as subordinates: "We can take up the perspectives of others out of sheer necessity for survival, the necessity to anticipate others' needs in order to be a good servant or slave, for example. Women learn well to do this with men; slaves have learned well to do it with masters. To be the valuers that ethical caring requires we need to preserve in ourselves as well as value in others, a certain spiritual integrity."[7]

Card and Sarah Hoagland both articulate concern about the potential that a commitment to care will result in extreme self-sacrifice. And where the model for care has been motherhood, a concern for self-sacrifice is warranted. Relationality is essential to keeping the self in mind so that we can interrogate the relationship between motivation or disposition on the part of providers and their knowledge of recipients. But retaining the self who is the provider or caregiver as integral to the caring relationship is critical for another set of more explicitly political reasons. In this vein, I would contend that a relational epistemology is a necessary precondition for attentiveness to the politics of care and, in turn, to a democratic politics of needs interpretation.

I have argued that while much of the work on care begins by asserting its necessarily relational character, the attachment to empathy, where empathy is either (1) naturalized, or (2) rationalized so as to be compatible with impartiality, appears at odds with such a relational focus. A model of public care requires that care resist its association with either of these conceptions of empathy. The naturalized version of empathy presents Noddings's problem of the "inner circle," failing to interrogate the social and political sources of natural ties. It also often assumes that needs are transparent to the caregiver in the context of these empathic relations. Where empathy is rationalized, the particular relationship between caregiver and cared-for is irrelevant. In both cases, Code's question, "Is 'S' in a position

7. Card 1990, 106–7. Bubeck also argues that we have to distinguish between the caring attitude and the cognitive function of care. With respect to empathy, she writes, "'[A]pprehending another person's reality' may be common to these various purposes, but the attitude itself is distinct: in managing or manipulating others the cognitive function is used for different purposes, usually for the purposes of people other than those whose reality is apprehended, while in caring such 'receiving' of others, as Noddings often calls it, is part and parcel of a benevolent relation between carer and cared for which compels the carer to act on behalf of the other person rather than in her own interests" (1995, 154).

to know?" is depoliticized. In the first case, the answer yes is taken for granted. In the second case, the question is viewed as irrelevant because on a rational model of knowing (liberal/positivist), the position of S is irrelevant. Anne Phillips has described such moves as the "arrogance of those who thought that ideas could be separated from presence" (1995, 8). And such arrogance has political consequences; it is most likely to occur, as Code notes, in situations of inequality:

> Where there is a difference of power, knowledge, expertise, a claim that I "know just how you feel" can readily expand into a claim that I will tell you how you feel, and I will be right, even though you might describe it differently, for your perceptions are ill-informed and my greater expertise must override them. Monologic, unidirectional epistemologies, where propositional knowledge claims are uttered by a "subject" about an "object" (S knows that p), legitimate such moves. (1995, 131)

As the case studies demonstrated, the position of those making knowledge claims, whether the knower is a "bougie" outsider or a community member is viewed by the "target population" as just as relevant as what they claim to know.

Code's alternative epistemology focuses on the explicit conditions of the knowing subject. In assessing knowledge claims, Code argues that "epistemic location" — that is, whether someone is in a position to know — is a critical consideration. The staff at the Beacons clearly didn't feel outsiders were in a position to know either the needs of their community or the best strategies for meeting those needs. The standards by which an epistemic location is judged to be adequate to knowing are relational, but not just relational to object (neutrality, distance, impartiality — the conditions of the social scientific knower, for example) but to subject; that is, the conditions of knowing have as much to do with identity of the knower. Code pushes the relevance of the question, Could he or she, in particular, have known that? And the standards for assessing the claim include the knower's relationship to the context and identities in question. This prompts her to advocate a dialogic approach to knowledge claims, an approach that resists closure and invites conversation, an approach she also suggests is necessary to "beneficent empathy." Such an approach is best facilitated in the context of face-to-face relations. Code's argument resonates well with the concerns of many recipients that experience in the community was critical. "Beneficent empathy" suggests that the disposition of the knower toward the known is relevant—that one's disposition toward the other shapes judgment in part by shaping perceptions. The contrasting conceptions of community illustrated in the Beacons interviews demonstrate that perceptions of the community were dependent to a large extent on one's status as community member or outsider. Experience living in the community and identity as a member of the community were the conditions Beacons staff considered relevant for knowledge claims.

There is much feminist work suggesting a need to be wary of experience as the authoritative basis for knowledge claims. Kathleen Jones argues:

> All too frequently the assertion that experience produces knowledge whose meaning is controlled by the experiencer/knower has defined experience in possessive terms. Only I who have an experience can know (own) what it means. Experience, thus, becomes the territory of personal identity, and personal identity becomes the basis for feminist epistemology and politics. (1993, 213)

Jones understands that the appeal to experience as the source of authority is motivated by an emancipatory politics, a politics that seeks to liberate experiences from the "colonizing effects of master discourses which have so far invalidated them" (214). Yet she argues that such a strategy fails to recognize the way in which a struggle for territorial sovereignty over experience may limit the potential to challenge existing paradigms of power and authority. Jones's work raises some critical questions about the extent to which we can comfortably talk about a single "women's experience." But she recognizes that there are risks in recognizing the diversity of everyone's experiences as well. She asks, "If everyone is speaking for and about herself, then how can we articulate, without subverting this practice, any collective goals?" (217).

I think Jones's analysis offers us some insight into the case studies. "Experience in the community" was invoked by recipients as the basis for authoritative knowledge about needs. Experience belonged to (was possessed by) recipients rather than providers. In this context, experience was an epistemological challenge clearly intended to have political consequences. While Jones fears that ultimately the turn to experience as the basis for authority will produce either essentialism, on the one hand, or a fragmentation that unravels the prospects for collective political action on the other, in the context of the case studies the dangers of either seem remote. In saying this, I do not mean to suggest that Jones's concerns are unfounded. Rather I am arguing that the turn to experience at this particular historical juncture is still embedded in an emancipatory politics without having been either institutionalized so as to reify its authority or fragmented enough to defeat the challenge to authority.

Timothy Kauffman-Osborne describes the emancipatory potential of invoking experience in the following terms:

> To deny the claims of experience is to fall prey to the seduction that defines the complex of masculinist discourses situated at the heart of the Western philosophical tradition. The thread connecting those discourses is their common subjection of everyday experience to rule by reason's reified abstractions. Should the day come when theory no longer impugns experience's capacity to take part in exploring the conditions of its own sense, then perhaps we can take our leave of this concept. (1993, 142)

He goes on to cite Dewey along the same lines:

> When the varied constituents of the wide universe, the unfavorable, the precarious, uncertain, irrational, hateful, receive the same attention that is accorded the noble, honorable and true, then philosophy may conceivably dispense with the conception of experience. But till that day arrives, we need a cautionary and directive word, like experience, to remind us that the world which is lived, suffered and enjoyed as well as logically thought of, has the last word in all human inquiries and surmises.[8]

While both Kauffman-Osborne and Dewey are reacting to a denigration of experience in the Western philosophical tradition, their arguments have relevance for the case studies presented here. Both Jones and Kauffman-Osborne acknowledge that experience may serve a strategic purpose at particular times and in particular contexts. Experience is being used to call attention to much of what is absent in the bureaucratic assessment of needs, absent in what Jones might refer to as "master discourses," which surround this process of assessment. In the context of claims to care, rela-

8. Dewey 1981, 372, quoted in Kauffman-Osborne 1993, 142.

tionships of power and domination tend to be cloaked by the supposed neutrality of knowledge claims and the supposed benevolence of providers.

Among other things, domination in the course of care relationships comes about in the course of defining needs, and in particular in the assertion of knowledge claims about needs. For example, the tendency to rely on "impartial experts" in the course of determining needs is a consequence of determining what kind of knowledge counts. As suggested in my analysis of the case studies, what kind of knowledge counts is intimately linked to *whose* knowledge counts. Again and again the staff at the Beacons suggested the offensive nature of traditional programs, professionally run by those from outside the community. In this context the invocation of experience as the basis for knowledge claims is part of an emancipatory struggle.

Leaving aside the actual motivations of those behind these programs, we are still confronted with the fact that their efforts were interpreted by community members as a form of sophisticated condescension and that community members saw such efforts as at best misguided benevolence and at worst open attempts at social control. Both of these facts are relevant. The success of programs by even the most traditional definitions of success is influenced by the presence or absence of trust, the sense of shared membership in the community, or a community boundary that marks one as an outsider. If levels of distrust are high — for example, if the community designated "at risk" knows that the agenda of the Casey Foundation is not their agenda — even the minimal level of cooperation required by "dependents" in paternalistic models of care is threatened. The position of those providing care is relevant in all these ways. In the following chapter I suggest how we might reconceptualize the practices of care to take account of this.

The claims of a provider to "know the needs of recipients" are critical to legitimizing the privilege of providers in the process of interpreting needs. In this sense a relational model of knowing that acknowledges compassion as relevant to caring but resists equating compassion *for* with knowledge *of* challenges the privileged position of providers. The case studies documented a consistent sense among recipients that knowledge claims on the part of providers ought to be challenged, and a strong sense that the knowledge that came with experience ought to be validated.

This epistemological shift has resonances with many of the concerns Solomon raises. What it means in the practice of care is the possibility of recognizing relationships of domination. If we think of care as addressing needs, and we think of it as therefore always involving some claim about what those needs are, we can see the relevance of thinking through what counts as legitimate knowledge claims of this kind. And where empathy is conceived as emotional displacement or putting oneself in the place of another, this move often works to perpetuate the power of professionals, replacing the voices of the subjects of care with the voice of the caregiver, with little recognition that there could be dissonance between these voices.

Selma Sevenhuijsen makes the connection between empathy and paternalism in the following terms:

> There is a great risk of paternalism or maternalism connected to the assumption that a single (hypothetical or actual) person could reach the "true" moral judgments. Moral judgments of course are dependent on interpretation. "Empathy" in itself forms no guarantee that someone's moral considerations are free of projection or misconception. The promotion of empathy is in itself insufficient to break the dominance of cognitive processes, in which "others" are objectified, and along with this the sexism, classism, and ethnocentrism in dominant currents in Western philosophy. For this to happen it is "necessary that the so-called "others" speak for themselves. "Listening," "communicating," "interacting" and "understanding" are more important cognitive elements of an ethics of care, seen in this way, than "empathy," just as the encouragement of pluriformity and compromise, in my opinion, is a better aim of moral debate than the creation of consensus. (1998, 156)

It is for these reasons that I turn in the next chapter to make the case for a democratic politics of care.

This chapter raised issues regarding the role of affect and cognition in knowing, challenged the traditional understanding of emotion, and raised questions about the proper conditions for knowing. The discussion of Solomon served to challenge the idea that emotions are a threat to making accurate knowledge claims by suggesting that we see emotions as species of judgment. Questions regarding the relationship between affect and cognition are not merely epistemological, for the notion that emotions are species of judgment may broaden our understanding of what counts as legitimate deliberative expression, a concern that I will address in the following chapter.

6

The Problem of Knowing Needs

A Case for a Democratic Politics of Care

The two previous chapters suggest that the project of bringing justice as impartiality together with the practices of care may be conceptually problematic and politically unhelpful. And yet I have acknowledged that I am sympathetic to the political concerns that motivate many of these attempts. This chapter argues that a reconceptualization of the paternalism critique, one that understands paternalism as speaking for others in the process of defining needs and suggests locating care within a deliberative democratic context, might be a more helpful way of addressing concerns about domination in the course of public care.

In brief, I will argue that many of the familiar versions of paternalism replicate the problem of impartiality presented in the discussion of justice. Work that criticizes paternalism as a violation of the rights of self-regarding individuals ultimately makes the practice of care unhelpfully problematic. Work that justifies paternalism, positing an "all-knowing paternal-ist" — like versions of care that treat empathy as compatible with impar-tiality — are conceptually incompatible with care as a practice sensitive to particularity and context. As a consequence, these versions of paternalism are also inadequate to take account of political problems that arise in the practice of caring — problems like distrust and the dilemmas of negotiating community boundaries. As the case study suggests, these are critical issues that current frameworks for policy making leave largely unaddressed.

By reconceptualizing paternalism so that it is seen as speaking for others in the social process of defining needs, we can see as relevant questions like: Who participates in this process of defining needs? Or, as Lorraine Code prompts us to ask, Are those who participate in a position to know needs in this community? If we are concerned to develop a paternalism critique that can serve as a guide for practice, it must allow us not only to identify the problem of domination but also to suggest an alternative. We must be able to recognize the possibility of domination or distrust without precluding the possibility of collective responsibility and, specifically, more mutual relations of caretaking. My reconceptualization of paternalism lo-cates the paternalism critique within a set of social practices, namely, the political process of defining needs. On this account, paternalism is a more genuinely political critique, one that, I will argue, implies a democratic politics of care as its alternative.

The Paternalism Critique

We will begin by exploring the inadequacies of familiar versions of pater-nalism. In these versions, paternalism is understood in terms of injustice. The political implications of labeling practices "paternalistic" have changed over time. Against the backdrop of traditional social hierarchies, hierarchies conceived as natural and supposedly unchallenged, paternalism was itself considered natural.[1] However, the contemporary version of pa-ternalism denies the inevitability of a natural hierarchy in roles, at least in the political realm. Instead, it conceptualizes legitimate social and political relations largely as the consequence of the consent of equal, autonomous individuals. This contractarian conception of the self is central to the mod-

1. See Sennett 1980; Fraser and Gordon 1997.

ern justice tradition. Against the historical backdrop of feudal forms of societal organization, the political organization coinciding with this was clearly liberatory in an important sense. But I argue that the understanding of *liberatory* as "free from intervention" — that is, the emphasis on autonomy as independence — ultimately devalues care.[2] In such a context, when institutional practices of care do develop, they evolve paternalistically. For here care always implies a less than fully autonomous recipient, a "dependent." Judith Shklar describes paternalism in terms particularly relevant for this project:

> Paternalism is usually faulted for limiting our freedom by forcing us to act for our own good. It is also, and possibly more significantly, unjust and bound to arouse a sense of injustice. Paternalistic laws may have as much consent as any other, but what makes their implementation objectionable is the refusal to explain to their purported beneficiaries why they must alter their conduct or comply with protective regulations. People are assumed to be incompetent without any proof. The result may be entirely just, but the treatment of the "clients" is not. Welfare recipients who receive benefits in kind rather than money are simply presumed to be incapable of understanding their own interests, "noncompetence is assumed until disproved." (1990, 119)

Shklar goes on to add: "The cognitive inequality between agents of the state and their clients is taken to be so great as to be unbridgeable as well as permanent. Whether they are to receive medical treatment, to be relocated, or given benefits in kind and monitored for compliant behavior, they are never owed nor do they receive an explanation for what is being done *for* them" (119).

Thus paternalism, by implicitly denying independence, or the competencies required for it, denies a characteristic critical to citizenship and becomes a political dirty word. So formulated, the conventional version of the paternalism critique is very good at recognizing such domination as injustice. But it simultaneously seems to prohibit collective responsibility

2. Nancy Hirschmann has argued that the contractarian vision of freedom as negative freedom might be understood as "non-dependence." This suggests why it is so difficult to treat those designated as dependents as full citizens. Freedom is understood as the precondition for full participation as citizen. See her work in *Rethinking Obligation: A Feminist Method for Political Theory* (1992).

generally, and specifically more mutual relationships of care. Here the recognition of domination as injustice rests on an equation of respect for self-regardingness with economic self-sufficiency and independence.

Paternalism becomes a political dirty word only in the context of such a particularly modern contractarian notion of the self. This vision of the self as basically rational and autonomous, and therefore equal in the terms of membership in the state, is not merely theoretical — represented in the work of thinkers like Immanuel Kant and John Rawls as well as Lawrence Kohlberg. It is an important political tradition that has shaped American economic, political, and legal institutions and in so doing has circumscribed practices within these institutions. Of particular interest for this project, it is a political tradition that has created reverence for the wage earner and disdain for those dependent on public care. Hence the assumption of "cognitive inequality" that Shklar identifies.

The familiar versions of the paternalism critique imply an emancipatory politics in their rejection of an assumption of natural hierarchy. But ultimately these accounts of the paternalism critique end up defining freedom and caring oppositionally. Like the justice framework explored in Chapter 3, these familiar versions of paternalism begin from a conception of the rational, autonomous, rights-bearing self, which makes problematic the valuing of care. Allen Buchanan argues:

> It is plausible to contend that the strongest arguments against paternalism must be rights-based arguments. Such arguments, if successful, would show that paternalism is unjustified because it violates individuals' rights. . . . General rights are said to accrue to persons independently of their participation in certain voluntary interactions and independently of their standing in certain special relationships to others. (1983, 76)

Again, as the discussion of the ethic of justice more generally suggested, positioning rights as independent of contexts of "interaction" and "relationships" makes rights-based concerns incompatible with the practice of care. Buchanan goes on to say that "claims of right are characteristically thought of as 'trumping' considerations of welfare, whether it be the general welfare or the welfare of the right holder himself" (78). Where paternalism is defined as violating such rights, the commitment to respect rights "trumps" the concern for care.

How then do we avoid the problem of domination that Buchanan's

rights-based argument is effectively resisting without allowing these concerns to outweigh those of care? In the following section I suggest that
John Stuart Mill may provide some guidance in this project.

Paternalism—Is It Ever Justified?

The work of John Stuart Mill is an implicit, if not explicit, foundation of
much of the contemporary concern about paternalism. Positions like the
one Buchanan describes—a strong libertarian opposition to paternalism—
are often attributed to Mill. It is not my intention here to offer a close or
comprehensive reading of Mill's work. Instead I will present a brief account of his work, focusing particularly on his defense of nonintervention
and his special case of justified intervention, then go on to review appro-
priations of Mill in the contemporary paternalism debate. I read Mill as
offering a two-pronged defense of nonintervention, and I find part of his
defense helpful in reconceptualizing the paternalism critique.

Mill argues that intervention in acts understood as self-regarding can
rarely be justified:

> But neither one person, nor any number of persons is warranted in
> saying to another human creature of ripe years that he shall not do
> with his life for his own benefit what he chooses to do with it. He is
> the person most interested in his own well-being. . . . With respect
> to his own feelings and circumstance, the most ordinary man or
> woman has means of knowledge immeasurably surpassing those
> that can be possessed by anyone else. The interference of society to
> overrule his judgment and purposes in what only regards himself
> must be grounded on general presumptions which may be alto-
> gether wrong, and even if right, are as likely as not to be misapplied
> to individual cases, by persons no better acquainted with the cir-
> cumstances of such cases than those are who look at them merely
> from without. ([1859] 1956, 93)

In many of the contemporary interpretations of Mill's paternalism, it
would be difficult to overestimate the commitment to nonintervention as
the best strategy for avoiding paternalism. Mill's distinction between self-
and other-regarding has been appropriated as a defense of a libertarian

interpretation of paternalism. Rarely is Mill invoked by contemporary commentators in defense of intervention. When, if ever, is intervention justified according to Mill? He argues that interference is justified in the case of a man selling himself into slavery:

> The reason for not interfering, unless for the sake of others, with a person's voluntary acts is consideration for his liberty. His voluntary choice is evidence that what he so chooses is desirable, or at least endurable to him, and his good is on the whole best provided for by allowing him to take his own means of pursuing it. But by selling himself for a slave, he abdicates his liberty; he forgoes any future use of it beyond that single act. He, therefore, defeats in his own case, the very purpose which is the justification of allowing him to dispose himself. (125)

These two formulations of the tension between interference and liberty resolve themselves in contrary ways, raising questions about how we understand "utilities of liberty," whether deferring liberty is a "rational calculation," and whether such a consequentialist defense of paternalism is consistent with liberal commitments to individual freedom of choice. Justifications for paternalistic intervention seem to require that we emphasize the utilitarian side of this tension. This is the tack he takes with respect to slavery, for it is not choice itself but what choice protects (that is, future choices) that Mill seems to value here. These are the standards (utilities) external to the process of choice itself that justify choice. Choices inconsistent with those standards are legitimately subjects of intervention. This aspect of Mill's argument has been much discussed, and I have little new to add. Instead, I would like to examine more closely his case for nonintervention.

It is helpful in illuminating the tension between utilitarianism and liberalism to focus on the way liberty and knowing are framed in relation to one another. Mill's argument for noninterference connects interest to knowledge, arguing that both are highly particular: "He is the person most interested in his own well-being. . . . With respect to his own feelings and circumstances, the most ordinary man or woman has means of knowledge immeasurably surpassing those that can be possessed by any other." Given this, it seems legitimate to ask, Can "those who look at them merely from without" ever make the kind of calculations that are required to justify interference for others? Mill seems to believe that even where we are "right" about the preferences of another, our "general presumptions" are likely to be "misapplied" to the particular individual cases.

Knowing Needs: The Idealized Paternalist

This part of Mill's argument would seem to be the ultimate defense of nonintervention. Yet later Mill seems to prescribe the exercise of individual autonomy for the pursuit of a specific good — that is, more liberty. Choices inconsistent with this end invite interference. But can we "know" that more liberty equals "best interest" for each and every individual? Mill seems to criticize intervention for what I will argue are two distinct — that is, separable — reasons: both because it violates individual choice as the expression of the value of liberty, and because the knowledge in which choice is based is highly particular, and therefore intervention would most likely be "misapplied." I will argue that it is necessary to disentangle these two claims in order to reconceptualize paternalism. Where nonintervention is defended as respect for choice, where choice is conceived of as freely willed apart from social constraints (and on some interpretations, this is Mill's meaning of self-regarding), the paternalism critique becomes the basis for opposition to all forms of intervention. Alternatively, where nonintervention is defended as respect for choice as a consequence of particular knowledge, knowledge particular to the individual in question may become the basis for an argument in favor of individual input into collective decision making. This distinction is critical to a democratic politics of care.

But it is important to emphasize the way in which this second justification for respecting individual choice has to be linked to *particular* knowledge in order to be connected to participation rather than nonintervention. If choice is respected on the basis of knowing, but knowing is conceived as "expert" knowing, then respect for choice can again be reduced to respect for "right" choices as expertly determined. On this account, the principle of nonintervention is replaced by paternalistic intervention.

Take, for example, Donald Regan's essay "Paternalism, Freedom, Identity, and Commitment" in which he lays out succinctly the tension between traditional utilitarian and liberal approaches to paternalism. Paternalism can be justified in a traditional utilitarian approach only if it will result in more pleasure or happiness overall for the person coerced. But this formulation ignores another value that need not be the same as happiness or pleasure — the value of choice itself. In an attempt to resolve this conflict, Regan argues that we might consider the question of when coercion would be justified from the point of view of an *idealized paternalist*. He defines the idealized paternalist as

> one who not only knows everything about the individual he is co-ercing and the consequence of various choices by that individual but who also has at his disposal means of coercion that can discrim-inate perfectly between different individuals and different acts. My hypothetical paternalist does not make mistakes; he need not worry about possible overbreadth in general prohibitions; and he operates in a system in which paternalistic legislation had no bad effects on the administration of the legal system generally. I am ignoring se-rious practical problems, because it seems to me that before we can decide what sorts of paternalism are justified in practice, we need to have some idea of what sorts would be justified for my ideal pater-nalist. (1983, 114)

The very idea that such an idealized paternalist could be a helpful theo-retical device in thinking through justified versus unjustified paternalism derives from specific assumptions, many of which I have already chal-lenged. The idea that relevant knowledge can be disembodied in this way is contestable, as both the case studies and the critique of impartiality dem-onstrate. As a *hypothetical* position, the ideal paternalist is allowed perfect knowledge and denied particular identity. But in the *act* of intervention, the actual intervenor always has an identity, and this identity is clearly relevant. It is relevant for several reasons, but the most obvious is that in the act of caring, the identity of the caregiver will be important to how those in the position of recipients interpret and receive the act of caring itself. Whether those who intervene are interpreted as disposed to "care" or to "exploit," we interpret their actions as paternalism or manipulation correspondingly. This is again illustrated by the case studies, where the relevance of identity (insider or outsider) to issues of trust, commitment, and suspicion in the practices of care was evident. If those who provided care were regarded as outsiders, this clearly made a difference to whether the intervention was generally regarded as care or manipulation.

Regan's idealized paternalist cannot be modified or amended to take account of concerns such as these. The relevance of a historical relation-ship between caregiver and care receiver, its influence on issues of trust,

and the interpretation of the disposition of care providers requires acknowledging paternalism as a relationship in the first place. But the idealized paternalist, situated by definition outside of any particular context,
has no affective ties that bind him or her to the process of caring for, or
committing to meet the needs of, others. It is exactly the function of the
idealized paternalist to make particular relationship irrelevant to the decision to intervene, and to make only certain kinds of facts about the situation count in justifying this intervention.

Knowing Needs in Political Practice

Regan's argument demonstrates a conception of the paternalist as a kind
of expert; it is ultimately this vision of justified paternalism that has been
the foundation for practices of care like those in New Futures. The case
study of New Futures seems to demonstrate both paternalism and its dangers. Despite sometimes very explicit directives to include those designated
recipients of care in the course of policy making, ultimately recipients of
care were taken seriously neither as a resource for knowing or meeting
needs nor as fellow participants in the process of defining needs. To be in
need is to require others to meet needs, and having violated the standard
of autonomy prerequisite to citizen participation, the "needy" are excluded. Repeatedly, the process of interpreting needs was dominated by
service providers and experts, despite the fact that they often lacked
knowledge critical to meeting their own Foundation goals.

Yet to invoke the paternalism critique in its conventional form in order
to identify this practice of domination, we run the risk of precluding public
social provision altogether. It is as if on this account of paternalism we
have two choices, either: (1) we accept that there is a needy target population, but the very recognition that this population is "needy" (as opposed
to self-sufficient) seems to require paternalistic caring and so precludes
more egalitarian forms of care; or (2) we refuse to recognize the needs of
this population as requiring collective social provision, and therefore deny
care altogether. On neither account is a more egalitarian model of care
possible.

To illustrate the dilemma, we might return to the case studies. Through
the course of interviews with those in the designated target population as
well as with policy makers, what became clear was that "needs" them-

selves were contested. One example that illustrates this well is the planning process for a Family Resource Center in Savannah. Those working with the city in policy positions emphasized the role of the Resource Center as locating social service intake personnel in the geographical vicinity of the community itself. By contrast, residents hoped for a community center that would be a center for activities such as dance classes and cultural activities, basketball and youth soccer leagues. They emphasized the need for the center as a place for the healthy as well as the struggling to congregate. When they talked about services, they focused on actual material resources: they wanted a kitchen and food, not AFDC intake personnel. They also wanted the center staffed by residents themselves. What the neighborhood "needed" was clearly contested.

The Beacons projects might be a model for a center along the lines desired by Area C residents. Those I interviewed who were involved with the Beacons repeatedly contrasted their program with the paternalism implicit in more traditional social service design. They argued that this paternalism was both offensive and misguided. As an alternative, they explicitly invoked a more democratic politics of needs interpretation—a process in which outsiders who come into the neighborhood saying, "OK, these are the problems we've seen. OK, this is what this neighborhood needs, without asking for the community's input and things like that," are rejected as legitimate sources of information. Alternatively, Beacons participants argued that "it's crucial that the community does its own needs assessment. You can't have someone come in from bougie town up there and say . . . 'I think this is the solution.' "

Behind the commitment to the community doing its own needs assessment is a strong sense that trust between knower and known is relevant to knowing "well." As Phyllis Rooney suggests, "Knowing what it is to know well requires an appreciation of what it is to trust well. Even in what seem like the most formal or impersonal arenas of knowledge production (in scientific inquiry for example), knowers rely on intricate networks of epistemic trust, critique and acknowledgement" (1993, 28).

The Beacons adopted a strategy of assessment that made these networks visible. In this process of needs assessment, community members extend themselves to one another. Moreover, because outreach coordinators saw "neediness" as a function of a complex of social and economic structures, they tended to assume that people in need of some resources were also sources of others. They were aware that members, like the community itself, could be a source of strength. This recognition is crucial, for on this account needs are situational and contextual rather than attributes of character. Such a recognition facilitates a move away from the fixed division of labor assumed in most traditional models of care through social provision. It explicitly challenges the idea of a permanent class of care providers and a class of recipients of care.

The outreach coordinators at the Beacons argued that the fact of shared community membership allowed those they went out to talk with to feel comfortable with them. They pointed explicitly to the problem of distrust as a barrier to traditional service providers' understanding needs. Even outsiders committed to "helping" were thus often misguided in their efforts — "It's not that they don't want to help, they just don't know how." The implicit pathologizing of the community entailed in their model of care often prevented them from seeing strengths in the community as well as taking the voice of the community seriously. This is a critique of traditional programs I heard repeatedly voiced by Beacons members. It is a critique that seems to capture the practices of New Futures as well. Familiar faces from community-based organizations were less subject to suspicion and more likely to be trusted than were "outsiders" from "bougie town." And trust was critical to facilitating a participatory conversation about needs.

As an alternative to traditional approaches, staff at one Beacons program argued that they did not begin with a predefined understanding of what is needed: "I'm not being told, 'Go with a piece of paper and get me as many names as you can of people who need jobs.' I'm going out there asking, 'What do you need?' And they are telling me, 'We need jobs.'" Part of getting people to talk to outreach coordinators about what they needed was "getting people to feel comfortable with you." The coordinators argued that this comfort level was more easily established among fellow residents of the community but that it was also something they had to cultivate even with people they had known awhile. It was crucial that they not fall into the role of expert — the voices of residents themselves were vital; a democratic process of interpreting needs was integral to both understanding and meeting needs. In short, their identification with the community, their identities as members of the community, became a lens through which the community interpreted the disposition of coordinators and determined their trustworthiness. The coordinators were viewed as trustworthy, and this was critical to getting people to speak openly with them.

In examining some of the conceptual work both on paternalism and on care, I was interested in whether these theories could take account of the importance of identity and the process of identifying with community as well as the identity of the paternalist in situations of care. But I found that much of the work on care, as well as many of the contemporary versions of paternalism, fail to take account of the relevance of identity and the problem of trust. Both the "idealized paternalist" and empathy, at least as Okin (1990) uses the term, are conceptual locations from which assessing the needs of another is viewed nonrelationally — the identity of the paternalist or the knowing empathizer is considered irrelevant.

In the case of the work on paternalism, Regan begins his argument with an idealized paternalist, *basically a paternalist with perfect information.* He argues that such a theoretical device is necessary to understanding how paternalism works in practice, and in particular to discerning justified versus unjustified paternalism. Paternalism is justified only in the case where the intervenor rightly predicts the best interests of the subject of intervention. The idealized paternalist is required, in part, because when we begin with the autonomous individual as our normative starting point, the barriers to intervention must be set quite high, and in fact the justification for paternalism basically comes down to acts about which the subject of intervention has inadequate information. Here the relationship between the paternalist and the subject of intervention, the disposition of the intervenor to care or her intention to manipulate, is irrelevant because motivation is in general irrelevant.

Despite Regan's claims, such a conceptual version of paternalism seems unhelpful to understanding the actual practices of paternalism. The position of paternalist as idealized is constructed to make the very issues of the particular identity of the subjects of intervention, issues that were so critical in discussions with Beacons coordinators, irrelevant. Moreover, by removing the issue of "disposition toward," specifically the interpretation of that disposition on the part of the designated "target population," the criteria for intervention fails to take account of the affective ties to community and corresponding issues of trust that seem to be relevant in the case studies. Getting it right, knowing well, does seem to depend on networks of epistemic trust.[3] Thus, in assessing the adequacy of care, it is relevant

---

3. For an excellent discussion of the role of networks of epistemic trust, see Code 1991, especially chapter 5, where she discusses the relationship between trust and vulnerability and links them to the flow of information. She writes, "Trust involves making oneself vulnerable, granting other people access to, and even control over valued aspects of one's life, conferring

whether the provider is within or outside of such networks. Where providers are understood as outsiders, they face skepticism about their real motives for care, and even when those are understood as basically benevolent, they may well be dismissed as well-meaning but misguided. Their judgments, as Mill put it, "are as likely as not to be misapplied to individual cases by . . . those who look at them merely from without." For all these reasons, where the practice of care assumes an all-knowing paternalist as provider and dependents as recipients, it is unlikely to meet needs appropriately. In the next section I begin to reconstruct a version of the paternalism critique that may better take account of the problem of domination while simultaneously suggesting a democratic politics of care.

Reconceptualizing Paternalism

In order to make nonpaternalism compatible with care, we must relocate the paternalism critique within the practices of care so that it captures a relationship between actual rather than idealized paternalists and their subjects. Analysis of the case studies suggests that issues such as trust and community membership are relevant to the practices of care, but they go unrecognized in a model that sees only the problem of perfect information. Providers often assume that their benevolence is transparent and that when combined with this information, their good intention translates into helpful practice. Locating paternalism in the actual practices of care, we see that even the problem of intention has to be seen relationally, for whether providers saw themselves as having good intentions matters far less than whether they were perceived as such by recipients. The concern about manipulation or malevolence was often an obstacle to securing even the minimal levels of cooperation necessary for paternalistic care.

Focusing on care as a practice provides an opportunity to examine how trust (and distrust) influence the interpretive process. Furthermore, viewing paternalism as occurring in the social process of defining needs, we must take account of the problem of interpretation as one of translation between, as one case manager put it, "different worlds that speak different

---

on them the power as much to damage, destroy or misuse those things as to take care with them. People trust one another with their most intimate secrets. . . . It is a risky business, whose very imperceptibility enhances the risks. Conferral and acceptance of trust require second-person interdependence in its most open and fragile aspect" (184).

languages." Interpretation across community boundaries may be made much more difficult and the opportunities for domination much greater where there is a long history of discriminatory practices. These relationships of power are integrally related to the problems of "perfect" information. For to be in need of care, to be in the position of prospective dependent, is to be vulnerable, and, as Code reminds us, there are always risks for the vulnerable when they divulge information about themselves (1991, 184). In beginning with a formulation of the paternalism problem that derives from the question, What would the (hypothetical) paternalist with access to perfect information be justified in doing to care for the deviantly dependent (but normatively independent) subject? we miss the relevance of factors like trust, community membership, and history. We miss the problems of interpretation, because we fail to take account of care as a process, and specifically the interpretation of needs as a political process.

My understanding of paternalism suggests instead that the problem of paternalism be understood *not* as the problem of intervention in the lives of (self-regarding) others, but as speaking for others in the process of defining their needs. Such a definition of paternalism implies as its alternative a more participatory process of defining needs, where the discussion privileges the voice of those presently "in need" in the course of defining "need" and determining arrangements of resources to meet those needs. Thus, in this new definition of paternalism, the alternative implied by the critique is a democratic politics of care.

To this end, my contention is, first, that a more participatory politics of needs interpretation is a necessary if not sufficient prerequisite to more effective policies — that is, policies that are more appropriate to meeting needs as the community membership understands them.[4] It would also provide the opportunity to reshape the agenda to reflect concerns familiar to community members, if not to outsiders. In this sense, such a participatory politics might generate new or alternative goals. Second, participation in the process of defining needs has as a necessary (again, if not sufficient) prerequisite at least minimal trust among members of the forum for participation. This raises two further questions: How does community identity relate to trust and participation? and What is its relevance for a democratic politics of care? These issues are relevant to the practices of care but are made relatively invisible in contemporary frameworks for public care.

---

4. I elaborate the further conditions for a democratic politics of care in my concluding chapter.

Situating paternalism as a practice within the social process of interpreting needs makes such issues visible. In the following section I will try to outline the relationship between these concepts as well as to suggest their import for practices of care.

Trust, Identity, Community: Revising the Practices of Care

> Ultimately the most profound trust issue is a practical one; given that we cannot successfully communicate and cooperate without at least a moderate level of trust and given that so often, in so many ways, there are compelling grounds for distrust, how can we progress from a situation of warranted distrust to one of well-founded trust? (Govier 1992, 18)

It is trust in this practical sense that, as the case studies suggest, is critical to effective care. I want to begin, however, by drawing out a series of conceptual relationships that illuminate the problem of warranted distrust while suggesting directions for the move to "well founded trust." I want to explore the link between trust, paternalism, and participation.

To begin, an adequate version of paternalism is, like trust, at least in part dependent on a particular understanding of the disposition of the caretaker or the one who is trusted. I argued earlier that the caring element that was part of more traditional understandings of care has dropped out of our familiar version of paternalism. I have also suggested that the link between the modern understanding of the self—specifically, the contractarian understanding—and the neglect of care is critical. Jones (1993) argues:

> Embedded in this theory [social contract theory] was a particular conception of personhood. Social contract theory, which continues to shape much of the contemporary discussion of authority, treats individuals as abstract entities whose identity as members of groups or classes is inconsequential to their political standing. . . . At least in principle, the concept of the individual as an autonomous self is an abstract, disembodied idea that denies the political significance of all differences—of class and race, as well as sex. (236)

The contractarian self is an abstraction from the very differences, race and class, that seem to matter in the course of the case studies. Moreover, given this understanding of the self as normatively autonomous and self-suffi-cient, of relationships as products of rational calculations, the disposition to care, to act benevolently toward another, gets reduced to a slightly more sophisticated version of "self" interest. In other words, it is not a disposi-tion *toward* or *for* another at all. As David Rothman (1981) has suggested, this is the "knee-jerk" reaction that follows from the dominant minimalist understanding of the self.

While against the backdrop of the modern vision of the self we are cyni-cal about the possibility of care, we acknowledge that there is a difference of degree (at least) between those who might claim to care and those who could not plausibly make such a claim. It is, as discussed in Chapters 1 and 3, the existence of both claims that care is the motivation for action and, simultaneously, a deep skepticism about such a caring disposition that makes *paternalism* such a political dirty word.

In much the same way, trust makes relevant the disposition toward the trusted, for it is in part the interpretation of disposition that influences the way we interpret what others say and do. In trusting others, "we expect them to act in ways that are helpful, or at least not harmful to us."[5] Trust-ing becomes a filter through which we interpret the actions of others. Even when on first appearance the evidence suggests betrayal, if we hear that a trusted friend has acted inappropriately, we do not accept this evidence uncritically (Thomas 1990). In the case of both trust and paternalism, the interpretation of the disposition of those who *claim* to care or to be trust-worthy is relevant to the process of interpreting acts of care and trust. The contractarian vision of the self has reduced disposition, questions of mo-tivation, to rational self-interest, making us generally deeply skeptical of claims to "care." Yet intervention would not be interpreted as paternalism if the disposition of the intervenor claiming to care was read with suspi-cion; we would not call something an "act of betrayal" if it were not situated within a relationship of trust. The reading of disposition is rele-vant to making the distinction between paternalism and manipulation, be-tween disappointed expectation and betrayal.

Disposition, here, captures a relationship — one's disposition toward an-other. As opposed to seeing trustworthiness as a property of individual *character*, we might better understand it as a property of a *relationship*.

5. See Blum 1980; Thomas 1990.

The language of character, of moral character in particular, is usually used to describe an internal state that would be prior to, and would produce a particular kind of disposition toward, others. I want to resist this, rather seeing trust or distrust as a product of engagement, of interaction with others. Much of the literature on trust has suggested that the presence or absence of trust indicates something about the character either of the trusted or the trusting. I am going to suggest that it is more helpful to look at the process of assessing or interpreting "character" as a process within social and political relationships, than it is to begin by attempting to describe the content of a trustworthy character itself.[6] It is more helpful because it gives us a way of acknowledging the political causes and consequences of trust or its absence, to address Govier's call to "progress from a situation of warranted distrust to one of well-founded trust."

The conventional understanding of paternalism has been reduced almost exclusively to the idea of intervention because care, like trust, is a relational term and is difficult to accommodate within a politics premised on the modern, specifically contractarian understanding of the self. A model of paternalism that understands it as the process of speaking for others in the course of defining their needs suggests the importance of the relationship between the paternalist and those subjects of care. Interpretation is a process that involves both interpreter and interpreted, and where the interpreted are human subjects, it also involves a process of self-interpretation. The disposition of each participant toward the other is relevant to the process of interpreting needs as well as to the initial decision to participate in this process.

The New Futures programs began with a commitment to inclusive participation in their initial program design. Yet as we have noted, participation on the part of those designated "at risk" or their advocates was never realized. How do we explain this? Like our conventional understanding of paternalism, our conventional explanations for participation, or more specifically, lack of participation, tend to lose sight of this relational component. The dominant liberal vision of the public sphere is as little more than a forum for the sum of the expressions of individual voices — voices that

---

6. For a helpful discussion of socially situated judgment, see Smiley (1992). While her work focuses on our practices of blaming, the framework she develops for thinking about judgment is helpful to thinking about trust as well. Of particular importance for analysis of these case studies is her claim that judgments of blame — and here, I argue, judgments about who is to be trusted — are embedded within configurations of community and roles within those communities.

express preferences and opinions formed prior to this "public" moment of aggregation.[7] Such a vision is problematic in many ways. For our purposes, however, the significant inadequacy of this model is that it suggests little responsibility on the part of those who dominate or control the public sphere for accessibility to the public sphere. Rather, conventional explanations for nonparticipation in this model revolve around assessing the individual capacities of nonparticipants.

We can, for example, look at some of the analyses of participation that are prominent in the field of political science. Bernard Barber (1983) depicts the analysis offered up by theorists of democratic elitism in the following terms:

> The theory holds that political distrust in the US exists in the masses because they are ignorant, alienated (lack democratic values), or anomic (lack all values); that is, they are incapable of accurately discerning technical competence or fiduciary responsibility in the political sphere, or even worse, they lack the values that would make them care about such things. (72)

Such treatments of political trust have seen trust largely as a function of individual personality variables. There are many parallels between the literature Barber is critiquing and work that focuses on moral character as the source of trust. "Trustworthiness" becomes a personal attribute somehow distinct from a broader social context in which expectations are premised on socially defined roles and relationships of power.

It is worth thinking, at this point, about how it is that trust differs from predictability—for this distinction highlights the relevance of disposition and relationality to the issue of trust.[8] If trust is reducible to predictability, then we seem to have created the problem of Regan's ideal paternalist under a different name: trust becomes a matter of right action on the basis of perfect information, which allows perfect prediction. Lawrence Thomas (1990) suggests the following relationship between trust and prediction: "A prediction is a statement about what will occur in the future. Both prediction and trust share this feature in common as trust entails a species of prediction, although the converse is not true. In fact, prediction can render trust unnecessary" (238). Similarly, Thomas notes, trust can be dis-

7. Elster 1986; Mansbridge 1992; Young 1993.
8. For an extended discussion along these lines see Virginia Held's chapter, "The Grounds for Social Trust," in her work *Rights and Goods* (1984).

tinguished from reliability: "With trust comes reliability, but not conversely. The laws of nature are reliable but not trustworthy" (238). What more than reliability is necessary to trust? Thomas says that trust, as opposed to prediction or reliability, is relational: "[A]n object of trust must be aware at some level or another that it is being trusted or at any rate, that it is being regarded by others as trustworthy" (239). He writes,

> [W]e make ourselves vulnerable to others in terms of trust only if it is possible for them to act in exactly the ways in which we trust that they will not act. Trust is anchored in the belief that a person will choose not to perform the action that he has been trusted not to perform, rather than in the belief that he cannot perform it. Trust is unnecessary if the person is incapable of performing the action (or if it is highly improbable that he could perform it) and this is known. (245)

Thomas's agenda is to convince us that wholly rational moral selves are not properly the objects of trust. Trust is an issue where disposition is an issue. Moreover, autonomous selves, self-sufficient selves, are not properly the object of trust either. Trust is an issue where vulnerability is an issue.

We must be careful at this point not to reduce disposition again to unconstrained choices. The case studies demonstrate the way in which trust (and in turn suspicion or distrust) is a relationship structured within a social and historical context. In these cases, trust is filtered through the lens of identity — identity with the community designated "at risk." And that social process of designation is itself one of the factors that creates suspicion rather than trust between the community and outsiders, for it translates vulnerability into an institutionalized dependency.

This suspicion is not inevitable but is a consequence of social and political relationships. The case studies suggest that the affective ties that delineate who counts as an insider and who counts as an outsider, are not "natural" but rather are the product of these relationships. In Savannah, for example, the description of previous Foundation efforts as "getting us half way," provides a basis for understanding suspicions of the project, the fear that New Futures represented "just another bureaucracy," with an "us-versus-them mentality," had clear ramifications for people's willingness to participate. In the case of the Beacons projects too, "traditional programs" were the topic of much criticism among participants; the history of such programs in the community served as the backdrop for assessing all new efforts by "outsiders."

Having said this, prospects for working across community might sound bleak. Yet we must be wary of drawing the distinction between insiders and outsiders in overly simplistic terms. There were, for example, instances where outsiders were viewed as sharing an interest in common with those in the community designated "at risk" and some instances where outsiders were allies. Many of those I interviewed seemed to believe that evaluators like myself would be genuinely interested in hearing their criticisms of local collaborative policy; they may not have trusted us or the Casey Foundation to do what was needed, but they understood that evaluators and recipients shared an interest in figuring out what was inadequate about the current arrangement. And one community member involved in Guardians of the Culture said she felt she could rely on groups like the National Endowment for the Arts to share and support her agenda. She saw groups like the NEA as having a historically progressive orientation, and she saw them as potential allies in her own vision of progress. Again, this suggests that in the community, who counts as an insider and who as an outsider cannot be naturalized; neither race, nor ethnicity, nor geography by itself is adequate to understanding the relationships of trust or the possibilities for extending these relationships. Rather, these relationships must be located in a much broader social and historical context in which the intersection of race, for example, with institutional relationships of power is critically interrogated.

Trust is an important and neglected variable in thinking about the practices of care. The interpretation of disposition or motivation on the part of program designers is often crucial to the decision of community members to participate in such programs. The high rates of participation in the Beacons programs were frequently attributed to the fact that the community-based organizations that ran them were recognized as "insiders." The case studies illustrate the relevance of issues such as identity, community ties, and trust, and their relationship to participation.

But much of the contemporary work on care as well as the conventional version of the paternalism critique fails to account for the influence of such variables on the practices of care.[9] Reconceptualizing paternalism as speaking for others in the social process of defining needs provides a framework for the practices of care in which issues such as these may be made visible

9. Sevenhuijsen's work (1998) is a recent and important exception to this criticism.

and confronted. A politics of care centered on the dilemmas of interpretation would immediately confront the question of who is an appropriate interpreter. This too will be contextually relative; community history and identity will often be relevant. But in a democratic polity, democratic citizens are respected as appropriate interpreters. Recognizing the problem of domination and creating the possibility for more egalitarian relationships of care requires this turn to a democratic politics of public care.

Equality and Partiality: What Role for Justice? What Role for Democracy?

I began this chapter with an account of the familiar version of paternalism. This account of paternalism relies on the same account of selfhood as is laid out in the work on justice. Against this vision of the self and its derivative account of politics, *paternalism* is a dirty word because, as Shklar (1990) argues, paternalism is an injustice. But as I have suggested, to view paternalism as injustice seems ultimately to lead to a politics of nonintervention among equals and pathologized dependency among unequals. Thus, to avoid domination as a justice framework understands it, we give up the possibility of mutual or more egalitarian relationships of care.

This, it seems, is a result of the way justice understands equality, for it is understood as the equality of equally rational, independent selves. Such selves neither need care nor experience vulnerability; their autonomy is defined in opposition to dependency. But as Joan Tronto, Selma Sevenhuijsen, and Kathleen Jones have all argued, such equality of equally rational, independent selves can exist only among abstract individuals; for actual individuals exist within complex networks of material interdependence and epistemic trust. These networks are products of social and political practices; they are not, as I suggested in my critique of Noddings, products of natural affective ties. My concern is that, while my analysis of the practices of care suggests the relevance of such ties, justice frameworks make such networks invisible.

I recognize that many will be uncomfortable when I suggest that such ties or partialities are relevant to constructing more adequate practices of public care. We tend to view affective ties as biases that promote or defend parochial attachments that are inconsistent with a commitment to the public good broadly conceived, the source of solidarity in a liberal political culture. Sevenhuijsen (1998) argues, "Normative and impartial reasoning, which employs universal standards and which abstracts as far as possible from the definition of particularity and context, is assigned an important role in confirming unity and homogeneity" (46). And Marilyn Friedman notes, "As many moral theorists would put it, bias interferes with the equal consideration of all persons which defines the 'moral point of view'" (1993, 9). Critics might argue that while I have demonstrated that partialities *do* play a role in current practices of public care, I have not made the case that they *ought* to.

Yet if, as many have argued, genuine impartiality is unachievable, it is difficult to see how it can serve as a guide to practice. Friedman suggests that many of these methods for arriving at impartial moral judgments involve "extraordinary cognitive feats":

> It is true that these methods are presented as "hypothetical" or "fictional" in some sense or other. If such forms of thinking were thoroughly hypothetical or fictional, however, they could provide no substantive normative illumination whatsoever, not even to the theorists who author these methodological devices. If these methods for representing impartial normative thought are to provide us with genuine substantive insights into matters of morality or politics, then they must outline methods of reflection that are within the capacities of human beings to adopt. . . . Some of the methods specified to yield impartiality are obviously beyond the capacity of any person to achieve simply as an exercise of thought. (1993, 19)

She sees two basic practical problems with trying to achieve impartiality through hypothetically putting oneself in the place of others. First, what we know about the standpoints of most other persons "underdescribes" those standpoints: "Most people whose standpoints we have to consider for the purposes of normative thinking are strangers or mere acquaintances known to us only under limited circumstantial descriptions that underdescribe their personal standpoints" (21). And second, even where we might know the motivations or preferences, they may be "unfamiliar, alien, even despised" from our own standpoint (21). Here Friedman echoes my own concerns about empathy as impartiality. But Friedman herself does not give up on impartiality; rather, she reconstrues it as a matter of degree, probably never fully realizable by human beings and approachable only incrementally through the gradual elimination of partialities (31).

While I am sympathetic to Friedman's claim that we should begin with our partialities, to her claim that critical moral thinking is essentially an intersubjective exercise in which dialogue is central, I think we must ask, If genuine impartiality is unachievable, why does the rhetoric of impartiality retain its appeal? We turn to impartiality to ameliorate the undesirable impacts of partialities, of parochialism. Iris Young has argued that impartiality should be distrusted because it has been used in practice to cloak the political power of dominant social groups, in effect to protect rather than to challenge certain parochial interests.[10] Certainly the case studies in Chapter 2 illustrate that a vision of authority in the process of needs interpretation was linked to an ideal of expertise justified by reference to impartiality. In the case of one New Futures city, we might suggest that this claim to impartiality served to protect the power of "the same 200."

If we are genuinely interested in ameliorating the undesirable impacts of partialities, they must be recognized and negotiated (not imagined away) within the context of an actually existing (rather than an abstract or formal) equality of membership in a deliberative democratic forum. If we take Mill's defense of nonintervention as a defense based in the respect for particular knowledge, then knowledge particular to the individual in question may become the basis for an argument in favor of individual input into collective democratic decision making. Such a practice recognizes Friedman's dilemma of "underdescription" and takes steps toward remedying it by maximizing the social knowledge available to participants in decision making.[11] Such a collective process of decision making might well result in informed and appropriate public care, rather than a definitive position in favor of nonintervention.

Deliberative Democracy: The Fit with Care

The turn to deliberative democracy makes sense at this point for a variety of reasons. First, the deliberative turn grows out of many of the same criticisms of the liberal justice framework that appear in work on care.

10. Young 1986, cited in Friedman 1993, 37.
11. This is also a concern of both Young (1996) and Sanders (1997) to which I will return more directly in the next chapter.

Theorists of deliberative democracy tend to reject the abstraction of *homo economicus* as inadequate or inappropriate to politics. Benhabib's defense of a deliberative turn argues:

> [M]uch political theory under the influence of economic models of reasoning in particular proceeds from a methodological fiction of an individual with an ordered set of coherent preferences. This fiction does not have much relevance in the political world. On complex social and political issues, more often than not, individuals may have views and wishes but no ordered set of preferences, since the latter would imply that they would be enlightened not only about preferences but about the consequences and relative merits of their preferred choices in advance. (1996, 71)

A deliberative democracy, by contrast with the liberal model I have been describing, would insist on the capacity for formulating new positions in the course of discussion (Phillips 1995, 149). The capacity for formulating positions within deliberation is critical, because it is here that partialities must be negotiated. Benhabib argues that the process of deliberation would have the following features: first, participation in deliberations is governed by the norms of equality and symmetry: all have the same chances to initiate speech acts to question, to interrogate, and to open debate; second, all have the right to question the assigned topic of conversation; and third, all have the right to initiate reflexive arguments about the very rules of the discourse procedure and the way that they are applied or carried out (1996, 70). Such procedures could open up the space to contest currently accepted practices of care, definitions of need, and visions of autonomy. While there are a variety of models of deliberative democracy, Anne Phillips remarks, "The common core that characterizes theories of deliberative or communicative or discursive democracy is that political engagement can change initial statements of preference and interests" (1995, 149). It rejects representation as an act that simply presents a pre-given, unchanging interest. It conceives of governance on a model of direct engagement.

Again, this emphasis on a process of engagement suggests the compatibility of deliberative democracy with a politics of care. Moreover, in treating both the preferences and the identities of participants as fluid, deliberative democracies create the space for the recognition and reconstruction of difference and thus for the negotiation of partialities. Whereas, as Young notes, the universalist pretensions of justice often cloak parochial interests, here parochialism would be made visible and could therefore be challenged.[12]

Is voice alone in the context of a deliberative democracy enough to address the concerns I have raised about public care? Iris Young and Lynn Sanders have both suggested that even in a context committed to equal voice, some voices will be at a distinct disadvantage. Young's concern is that this deliberative negotiation may preclude certain forms of expression. While Young generally endorses deliberative democracy, she worries that our common notions of deliberation are too narrow to include all the forms of communication that legitimately persuade others in a situation of democratic decision making: "In the history of Western philosophy and political theory, a process of deliberation has usually been understood as disciplined and unemotional. The deliberative man rises above his impulses and feelings to consider impartially an issue on its 'objective merits'" (1996, 127).

Now obviously, if in invoking deliberation we reinvoke the ideal of impartiality, we have re-created the problem of the liberal justice model under a new name. Young insists that nondeliberative modes of communication, "expressions of passion, anger, depression, fear," are "often appropriate and necessary to enable people to recognize others in their concreteness" (1993, 129). In order to avoid the problem of abstraction that we critiqued in the account of Rawls, we must broaden our account of deliberation to include such communicative acts, for "even communication situations that bracket the direct influence of economic and political inequality nevertheless can privilege certain cultural styles and values" (1993, 126). Of particular concern, given the picture presented in the case studies, Young worries that "a deliberative model of democratic discussion tends to presume that participants in the public already understand one another, that they share premises, cultural meanings, ways of speaking and evaluating" (1993, 128). If this is indeed what we must mean by deliberation, then deliberative democracy would fail to recognize many of the differences that actual participants bring to the discussion.

Lynn Sanders is similarly concerned that "deliberation" tends to get equated with a limited range of expressive strategies. She argues that "ensuring participation in deliberation, and guaranteeing a discussion that

12. Joan Tronto has similarly argued that one advantage of caring is that "[c]aring calls attention to its parochialism whereas theories that claim to be universal cloak their parochialism" (1996, 148).

calls on all perspectives, is not just a matter of teaching everyone to argue" (1997, 367). Like Young, Sanders is concerned that deliberation is identified with the pursuit of common voice and that "[d]eliberation is a request for a certain kind of talk: rational, contained, and oriented to a shared problem." She continues, "Arguing that democratic discussion should be rational, moderate, and not selfish implicitly excludes public talk that is impassioned, extreme, and the product of particular interests" (370).

While Young criticizes deliberative democracy as assuming unity as a prerequisite to democratic deliberation and in so doing harboring mechanisms of exclusion, she argues for a communicative model open to forms of expression like storytelling as important forms of persuasion. Such a communicative process "maximizes the social knowledge available to participants in decision-making" (130). In broadening the communicative process, challenging traditional ideas about who has the authority to speak and what counts as legitimate speech, Young's communicative model of democracy addresses many of the concerns raised by the cases.

While the critiques of deliberation offered by Young and Sanders certainly apply to some models, not all theorists of deliberative democracy share the limited vision of deliberation they are critiquing. Anne Phillips reflects on Young's concerns and offers the following: "Though I take her point that deliberation may suggest an overly dispassionate kind of discussion between people who already share the same way of talking, the distinction she makes between deliberation and communication is not as important as the underlying areas of convergence" (1995, 149). I think the heavy emphasis Phillips places on the process of political engagement is consistent with broadening the account of deliberation to include rhetoric, storytelling, and testimony, to recognize different strategies of persuasion as legitimate. And Phillips explicitly rejects the claim that deliberative democracy must either start from, or produce, a consensus. "Deliberation matters only because there is difference," for as Phillips notes, "if some freak of history or nature had delivered a polity based on unanimous agreement, then politics would be virtually redundant and the decisions would already be made" (1995, 151). The democratic dialogue that is opened up does not guarantee consensus, but deliberation opens up at least some hope of increased mutual understanding. Such mutual understanding is a critical first step to the organization of more effective public care.

Yet if I am suggesting that partialities play a role in this dialogue, Is there not the risk that an equality that coexists with partiality will allow certain parochial interests to remain entrenched? What of the value of fairness? Is there no place for justice?

It is interesting that those who have taken care and justice seriously, while reluctant to give up justice, have also recognized the problems of compatibility. Joan Tronto argues, "We should note admitting care to our political framework is not meant to displace justice and judgments made on the basis of justice. Care does not require that we surrender a commitment to universal principles simply that we recognize that as they have been thus far constructed, they do not cover all possible conditions in the world" (1996, 148). And in fact, as we have seen, she argues that justice should play a critical distributive role with respect to care: "Obviously a theory of justice is necessary to discern among more and less urgent needs. Yet the kind of theory of justice that will be necessary to determine needs is probably different from most current theories of justice" (1993, 138). And while Shklar claims that challenging theories of justice is not her aim, she also acknowledges that "none of the usual models of justice offer an adequate account of injustice because they cling to the groundless belief that we can know and draw a stable and rigid distinction between the unjust and the unfortunate" (1990, 8). She goes on to add, "[N]o rules that we could invent would be better because we remain both too ignorant and too diverse to be fit into any single normative schema. We are strangers to one another and we are too ignorant to judge each other" (27).

Kathleen Jones argues that in the end compassion does not abandon rules or rights; instead, "it seeks to enrich these conceptions by detaching them and itself from private, possessive moorings" (1993, 244). Selma Sevenhuijsen echoes this concern about justice when she comments that in the context of the ethic of care "the moral situation takes on a different form than in the liberal ethics of rights. The ethic of care has its own moral vocabulary, which is able to incorporate certain elements of liberal ethics but which at heart has a different moral epistemology" (1998, 54). But again, in the spirit of Shklar, Tronto, and Bubeck, Sevenhuijsen is reluctant to give up on a role for justice:

> The question of the relationship between each of these vocabularies is, however, also from a philosophical perspective, much more complex. The answer depends to a certain extent on the particular variety of the theory of justice and particular version of the ethics of care which are being employed. However, in spite of this, it seems

clear that in a number of respects the feminist ethics of care offers a
radical alternative to the liberal justice idiom. The manner in which
moral subjectivity and moral situations are considered in the ethics
of care leads to a relational image of human nature which is incompatible with the atomistic, individualized subject of liberal political
philosophy. In my opinion, the feminist ethics of care employs a
moral epistemology which forms a radical break with epistemic rule
of liberal political philosophy. On the other hand, this does not
imply that I argue for a definitive farewell to liberal concepts such
as equality, justice and autonomy . . . on the contrary, it simply
means that they need to be re-thought from the perspective of the
ethics of care. (34)

There seems to be an ambivalence about whether justice can do the political work of ensuring nondomination.[13]

Of these accounts, it is Sevenhuijsen who goes the furthest in rethinking
justice. And as I argued in Chapters 3 and 4, there are good political reasons why we might want to hold on to justice in order to prevent domination. Sevenhuijsen's argument here dovetails nicely with the reconstruction
of paternalism that I am suggesting. For while I argue that the paternalism
critique is better understood as the problem of speaking for others, I am
trying to relocate the critique of domination — to see paternalism as incompatible with our democratic tradition rather than to focus on it as incompatible with our justice tradition (to focus on it as a rights violation). I
have already suggested in some detail why I see this as advantageous for
the project of public care: to see paternalism as a rights violation is to
invoke a vision of an autonomous, rights-bearing, moral subject where
autonomy, understood as self-sufficiency, precludes the possibility of care.

Sevenhuijsen too raises questions about the compatibility of justice and
care. She argues that needs are distorted in the vocabulary of justice: "In
the liberal framework, autonomy and independency tend to be conflated
and autonomy in the sense of autonomous judgment is linked to an ideal
of independence as self-sufficiency and to marginalization or even repres-
sion of the dependent dimensions of the self" (1998, 63). But she suggests

13. Phillips argues, "If we consider liberal democracy as an amalgam of certain key principles from the liberal and democratic traditions, what it takes from liberalism is an abstract
individualism, which may note the differences between us, but says these differences should
not count. At its best, this is a statement of profound egalitarianism that offers all citizens the
same legal and political rights regardless of their wealth, status, race or sex. At its worst, it
refuses the pertinence of continuing difference and inequality, pretending for the purposes of
argument that we are all basically the same" (1993, 114).

that autonomy, equality, and justice (as I have suggested paternalism) can be reformulated. Situating autonomy within the ethic of care "would replace the idea that dependency forms an obstacle to autonomy with the concept of interdependency" (1998, 139–40). Similarly, Sevenhuijsen is critical of equality as it is defined in relation to the justice tradition, for it is an equality of sameness.[14] This equality, she notes, is the equality of abstract rather than actual persons. The public sphere as the domain of rights and justice produces deliberations in which "we should abstract from who we are or want to be, and from the way in which interpersonal relationships actually proceed" (53). Sevenhuijsen argues for revising the arguments surrounding social participation, autonomy, and equality from the perspective of a communicative and relational paradigm that provides space for diversity and situated forms of subjectivity:

> Seen from this perspective, justice cannot be formulated as a standard set of norms and rules, be they procedural or substantive. Justice cannot be separated, any more than care, from the way in which we give shape to our social and political participation. Justice is a process in which content and form are interwoven in specific ways, or a common commitment to structure our collective lives in accordance with situational considerations on just rules and public provisions. . . . Justice, thus conceived, explicitly opens discursive space for deliberating about what counts as injustice or in other words for continuous reflection on which "social evils" we need to address. (145)

Such a concept of justice differs fairly radically from most current models; it is openly situational rather than abstract, it is thoroughgoing in its commitment to process, and it suggests that what counts as a social evil is identified in a process of dialogue rather than by direct recourse to universal principles or law. Such a concept of justice seems, in short, to turn on deliberation.

Deliberative democracy would open up avenues for recognizing and negotiating difference and diversity. In this sense, it avoids the problematic vision of "equality as sameness" that both Phillips and Sevenhuijsen identify. "When the norm of equality is interpreted as sameness," Sevenhuijsen writes, "we lose sight of the fact that it is necessary to reflect upon pat-

14. For a helpful account of the relationship between abstract individualism and liberal democratic understandings of equality, see Anne Phillips, *Democracy and Difference* (1993), especially chapter 2.

terns of 'othering' and the value attached to difference" (1998, 142). She continues:

> Equality in the tradition of contract theory posits that people have equal rights, in this case to care provisions. Compensation for inequality then becomes an issue for normative theory. Equality from the perspective of an ethics of care means recognizing the fact that everyone needs care, but also that equality can only be achieved by paying sufficient attention to the diversity of needs. The issue of normativity is then to be found in questions such as "how should we deal with plurality in care needs?"; "how can we guarantee that groups of people are not unnecessarily privileged in their ability to acquire care?"; and "how can dependency be given a place in thinking about necessary care?" (143)

A process of deliberative democratic engagement is critical to addressing questions such as these.

If we are to take the project of organizing a nonpaternalistic public care seriously, the turn to justice as traditionally conceived seems problematic. Yet if we respect the political impetus behind the desire to assure fairness, to ameliorate the negative effects of partialities, to cope with Friedman's problem of "underdescription," care does seem to require a democratic context. Phillips, in one of the most interesting moves of her argument for "a politics of presence," suggests that a process of democratic engagement rather than abstraction may actually be central to achieving equal consideration:

> With the best will in the world (and all too often we cannot rely on this), people are not good at imagining themselves in somebody else's shoes. We may get better at such imaginative acts of transcendence when our prejudices have been more forcefully exposed but this happens only when the "other" has been well represented. (1995, 53)

While impartiality or the acts of transcendence often required by justice may be impossible, we may (ironically) come closer by degrees to realizing the goals of fairness as *actual* equal consideration through a deliberative democratic process open to partialities. The concluding chapter suggests a preliminary outline for a democratic politics of care.

7

Institutionalizing a Democratic
Politics of Care

In this final chapter I offer a rough framework for institutionalizing a democratic politics of care. This project began by suggesting that our ambivalence toward care is a long-standing one, an ambivalence that precedes the contemporary welfare reform movement. The first chapter suggested that this attitude toward public care is rooted in the institutional traditions of our liberal political culture. In order to understand this ambivalence, we had to analyze the organization of public and private activities and the justifications for such organization. Of particular importance was the emphasis on the independent "self-made man" as public actor.

The second chapter used case studies to suggest that the corollary of the deserving "self-made man" is the denigration of "dependency," specifically the pathology associated with public dependency. This vision of dependency shapes practices of public care: those in need of care are also taken to be in need of authority.

Although critical of such paternalistic relationships, I was also wary of the political implications of the conventional critique. Paternalism is a political dirty word because as a public practice it violates other public commitments. But the conventional understanding focuses on paternalism as a violation of the rights of autonomous individuals. On this account, in order to avoid paternalism out of respect for rights, we may neglect needs altogether. I suggested that paternalism is a problematic practice, but I shifted my focus to argue that such practices of care are ultimately incompatible with our democratic commitment to equal voice. Domination, then, is understood as a failure to respect others as equal members of a democratic community rather than as a failure to respect individuals as autonomous rights bearers. And nondomination does not require nonintervention. I saw the Beacons programs as a hopeful alternative strategy for organizing public care. As such they offer important insights for rethinking the organization of public care.

Beginning with these case studies, I turned to work on the ethic of care to fill out an alternative vision. Because this work starts from the premise that needs (often as opposed to rights) should be central to our ethical decision making, it seemed appropriate to look to work in this field for guidance. However, despite the explicit commitment of much work on care to a focus on the actual rather than the abstract, the practical rather than the principled, much of this work failed to take account of the problems of care in political practice. Specifically, there was in some of this work an ironic tendency to essentialize need, to set it outside of politics. As a consequence, the actual processes of interpreting needs were made invisible.

As we have seen, others have worried about the inadequacies of care as a guide for public practice. Many of them have argued that care requires justice as a complement in order to serve as a more adequate account of morality. I examined work that attempts to bring justice together with care as well as work that claims care has always been a critical if neglected aspect of justice. I argued that the political concerns motivating these attempts to bring together justice and care often remain unaddressed. On the one hand, there is work that attempts to bring justice and care together as complementary but analytically distinct frameworks. I suggested that this work, at least when it invokes justice as it is conventionally conceived, was often both conceptually problematic and politically unhelpful. The turn here was often to distributive models of justice that commodified care in order to talk about its fair allocation. But care understood as a good fails to recognize the important process orientation of care—care understood as a relationship.

On the other hand, there is work like that of Susan Okin, which roots the compatibility of justice and care in a conception of empathy—the ability to put oneself in the place of others. The hope is to avoid the problematic partiality, the parochialism and exclusivity, of circles of care. This work attempts to bring justice and care together at the intersection of empathy, where empathy is understood as compatible with impartiality. In so doing, the critical contribution of much work on care, its attention to particularity and context, is lost.

To retain the relevance of context, we must reconstruct what counts as authoritative knowledge in the context of care. In Chapter 6 I suggested that an important political impetus for bringing justice and care together can be understood in terms of the question, Who has the authority to define needs for whom? The literature on paternalism offers some insight into the conventional approach to this question. But this approach begins by considering the problem of authority in the abstract—as a merely epistemological one. Justified intervention is intervention that would be condoned by the idealized paternalist, the paternalist with perfect information.

However, the problem of authority in practice is best understood as the problem of speaking for others, a problem that is *both* epistemological and political.[1] Returning to the case studies, the problem of speaking for others is complicated by the construction of dependency and its intersection with issues of identity, community, and trust. In light of this, I argued that the practices of care need revision.

In this chapter I argue that this revision requires both a democratic politics of needs interpretation and a democratic politics of care. This will require institutional reorganization. The problems of providing adequate care are inseparable from the organizational and social and political settings in which they arise.[2] I have thus far focused on illustrating the politics

1. For a helpful overview of "the problem of speaking for others" as both epistemological and political, see Linda Alcoff (1991).

2. For a similar argument concerning care in a hospital setting, see Daniel Chambliss, *Beyond Caring: Hospitals, Nurses, and the Social Organization of Care Ethics* (1996). Chambliss argues that often the way we talk about ethical dilemmas diverts attention from the structural conditions that have produced the problem in the first place (92). Such ethical problems are not, he argues, random or isolated failures of the system. Organizational and professional roles and settings are not made in some hypothetical "free choice zone": "The assumption of relatively autonomous decision makers is simply unrealistic" (182).

of needs interpretation in practices of public care, arguing that this politics is inconsistent with our public commitment to democracy. But a democratic politics of interpreting needs is only a start. What more is necessary to a democratic politics of care? Such a politics of care rests on an interlocking set of recognitions:

First, a democratic politics of care presumes that both the independent "self-made man" and the "welfare dependent" are myths. The needy are rarely defined as such because they have excessive needs. Rather, the politics of this distinction between the "self-made" and the "needy" center on the question of who meets their respective needs: Are these needs met privately in the context of the family or the economy? Or are they met publicly by the state? When we ask the question in this way, we come to see that we are identifying different relationships of *interdependence*. This challenges work that reduces dependency to issues of individual character, recognizing dependency instead as a description of social relationships. In Sevenhuijsen's terms, we must demand that the moral subject unlearn his denial of dependency (1998, 19). But we should be prepared for such demands to go unmet, for current conceptions of dependency are held in place by a relationship between providers and recipients that providers in particular may be reluctant to give up. In light of this, we must confront questions about the political organization of public care.

Second, having moved to a model that presumes interdependence, the roles of provider and recipient become fluid. Again, they are not roles derivative of individual character, but rather roles within relationships. Those in need at one point in time or place provide for others at another. And often the welfare recipient is simultaneously a provider of welfare for her family or her community. The case study of the Beacons demonstrates the possibilities for programs that view communities designated "at risk" as resources for, and not merely recipients of, care.

Finally, once we acknowledge that provider and recipient, cared-for and caregiver, are social positions rather than character traits, we can also distribute the work of care more or less equitably. The current organization of care in which some "care about" and others, usually women and people of color, do the work of care, could be challenged. Joan Tronto describes the usual division of labor as one in which "caring about and taking care of, are the duties of the powerful. Care-giving and care-receiving are left to the less powerful" (1993, 114). She continues:

Thus, "taking care of" is more associated with more public roles, and with men rather than women. Perhaps one of the most common usages of "taking care of" in American English language is the idea that by working at his job a man is taking care of his family. The doctor is taking care of the patient, even though the nurses, orderlies, and lab technicians are the actual providers of hands-on care. Race differences about care have been part of American political thought; especially recall the racist White view that African Americans were child-like and required that Whites "take care of" them, before, during, and after the Civil War.

Out of this association of "taking care of" with masculinity, "caring about" also becomes gendered, raced, and classed: men and people of privilege take care of; they care about public and broader issues. Women and people of color have very little to take care of, they care about private or local concerns. (115)

Construing provider and recipient roles as social rather than natural, fluid rather than static, disrupts this set of associations and is a necessary first step in contesting the division of labor. The authority of providers in the current processes of care is legitimated by reference to the dependency of their clients. Once dependency is normalized, we open up the possibility for democratizing authority. As both Tronto and Sevenhuijsen have suggested, the recognition of interdependence and the vulnerability associated with it may provide a different basis for equality.

The rejection of current constructions of dependency is critical both to effective public care and to democratic public care. Ultimately, there is a basic contradiction between dependence, understood as opposed to independence, and democratic empowerment. This conceptual contradiction has clear political implications: the best-intentioned policy recommendations that fail to recognize this contradiction will fail to accomplish meaningful empowerment.

To illustrate this conceptual tension and its implications for practice, we might look at another set of case studies. Joel Handler has long been concerned with the politics of welfare. In one of his most recent works, *Down from Bureaucracy,* Handler suggests that empowering recipients in the bureaucratic process is critical to improving the practices of the social welfare state. Handler is not naive; he is aware of how difficult this process of empowerment will be. But he provides several examples of "empowerment by invitation" that he sees as potential models. In the examples he uses, there are large differences in the power of the parties involved:

> If the weaker parties are to engage in genuine participation, they have to be empowered. . . . Power and empowerment are relational; both the powerful and the powerless have to perceive and experience reciprocal benefits.
>
> Where do the resources necessary for empowerment come from? In part the weaker parties develop the resources on their own; at the very least, they have to be active agents in appropriating to their advantage whatever resources are available. But it is my belief that in most situations, weaker parties cannot become empowered and maintain empowerment on their own — at least in the long term. Over time, the more powerful interests, especially bureaucracies, have too much command over resources. The stronger parties will reassert domination either coercively or by co-optation. Therefore, in order to maintain empowerment, the weaker parties have to get outside resources. In the examples described in this chapter, the resources come from the stronger parties themselves — hence, the expression empowerment "by invitation." (1996, 132)

In many ways, New Futures seems to be an example of such "empowerment by invitation." Yet as the case study suggests, participation in this setting was largely envisioned as a process of "buy-in" on the part of the community designated "at risk." My concern here is that it is difficult in Handler's examples to tell the difference between participation as "empowerment" and participation as "buy-in" or co-optation. This distinction is difficult to draw because the positions of provider and recipient remain largely unchallenged.

Handler acknowledges that the conditions of empowerment become much more problematic with human service agencies: "There is usually an asymmetry of information. In many situations, the official or bureaucrat has information that is not normally available to clients" (139). He also acknowledges that the "moral typification serves to disempower dependent people" (139). Yet he remains hopeful that empowerment can take place in a context where both bureaucracy and dependency are left unchallenged.

In a section entitled "Community-based Care," Handler celebrates empowerment by invitation in the context of adult day care: "Not only do clients share the work, they also become an important source of information. More information is generated . . . and it is of a different quality. There are now personal reports of quality of care rather than those made by an inspector relying on records and interviews" (145). But one can become a source of both labor and information without achieving what I understand as meaningful empowerment or "genuine participation." Empowerment by invitation does not necessarily translate into the power to participate as an equal in decisions about what to do with this information or how to organize the division of labor. Professionals are still setting the agenda. This is evident even as Handler argues for the success of "empowerment by invitation":

> The powerless have to be in a position to contribute something of value. In most of the examples, this was true. They contributed to professional or enterprise goals. When they cannot make a meaningful contribution, empowerment becomes problematic. . . .
>
> Despite the challenges, one can see progress with empowerment by invitation. . . . With "softer" human services, professionals have to come to realize that empowerment is not a zero-sum proposition, but rather that *their* professional task will be accomplished better with empowered clients. This sounds easier than it is in practice. After all, in medicine, genuine informed consent — as distinguished from merely obtaining the patient's signature on a form — is still the exception rather than the rule. Still, it somehow seems easier to try to persuade officials and professionals when the task starts from the proposition that they will be better off. (242–43)

My concern is that the "professional or enterprise goals" will not represent an agenda appropriate to the needs of recipients as they understand them. This is not the claim that professionals have got needs "wrong" and recipients have got them "right." Rather, it is the claim that these needs are embedded in a politics of interpretation that is currently bureaucratic rather than democratic. In such a context, where needs are contested the professional interpretation tends to win out without serious challenge.

Handler himself recognizes the obstacles here: "There are so many reasons why dependent people cannot participate, at least in a meaningful way. People who are poor, who lack resources, who are vulnerable, cannot be expected to challenge bureaucrats and professionals" (242). Empowerment by invitation seems to amount to the claim that when professional interests and client interests coincide, clients will be invited to the table; where there is conflict, they may not make the guest list at all.

Interdependence and the Possibility of Mutual Relationships of Care

A democratic politics of care requires a fundamental challenge to the professional-client relationship as it is currently institutionalized in the organization of public care. Does this mean that professionals have no role to play at all? The comments by Beacons staffers seem relevant here. As one director noted, "Everything filters down. If the design assumes pathology, that filters down. If you hire outsiders, you're not sending the message that the help is here in the community." With an awareness of this "filter down" effect, when staffers made decisions to "invite" professional service providers in, it was only after careful consideration and usually as a last resort. Most important, by contrast with Handler's model of empowerment by invitation, the role of guest and host were reversed. Here community members set the terms of engagement.

Elaine Martin contrasts such "mutual aid" organizations with both statutory services and traditional philanthropic services:

> The mutual aid or self-help organizations mentioned earlier present a quite different situation, with the members constituting the service providers, the service consumers, and the organization's authority structure. In this last category the hired professional is in the minority, the invited intruder dependent upon the favour of the organization. In the first two categories, statutory services and traditional voluntary services, this weak position belongs to the consumers invited to sit on a board or advisory committee. (1986, 187)

Martin, like Handler, understands that the obstacles to empowerment are high. Her insight is that the invited guest/intruder is always in the weaker position; empowerment from this position is difficult if not impossible. Martin's analysis suggests the possibility of an alternative institutional organization that would shift the balance of power. In such a situation, the professional becomes the occasional "hired help."

How do we foster such alternative institutional arrangements? While I believe the conceptual challenge to dependency is an integral part of the process of shifting the balance of power, I am under no illusions that a conceptual move translates easily or directly into political reorganization. While there are certainly examples of strong welfare rights organizations, there is no doubt that the resources to organize are unevenly distributed. Where traditional service providers are involved in supplying grassroots mutual aid organizations or community-based organizations with resources, funding mandates often ensure that the provider's vision of needs and care dominates; populations that receive assistance are held accountable to someone else's agenda. Yet in challenging the notion that good citizens are self-sufficient citizens, in beginning, as Mitchell and Sevenhuijsen suggest, by assuming *all* citizens are vulnerable, we challenge the connection between dependence and incompetence that legitimates strict accountability, opening the way for more flexible forms of organization.

While some may worry that too much flexibility in funding guidelines opens up the possibility for abuses, in the case of the Beacons, the flexibility has largely been seen as an asset: "The lack of eligibility constraints and rigid program requirements have fostered creativity, energy and the tailoring of programs and strategies to the needs of the school and communities. Where there is a strong agency flexibility this has enabled the Beacon to be responsible and innovative" (Cahill et al. 1993, 20). The report notes that this is not without its costs, for the local community-based organization here gives up the protection of recourse to rigid rules as a way of managing the political demands that accompany public funding (20). While a more traditional model of accountability might provide protection from such demands by clearly stating "the rules of engagement," it was clear from talking to directors of Beacons programs that from their perspective, the benefits of flexibility outweighed the costs. Rigid funding guidelines are often seen as necessary because of a lack of trust in the competence of those at the grass roots. If one assumes incompetence, that too filters down. In contrast:

> The choice for Beacons to be developed and managed by lead community-based organizations has brought many strengths to the initiative. The sector represented by community-based organizations offers much promise for finding solutions that meet the needs of disconnected youth and families under stress. Because their development has been rooted in communities and neighborhoods, many of these organizations have characteristics that are closer to the home

cultures of the children and youth they serve than schools or other formal service systems. Leadership in many community-based organizations tends to more closely represent the racial/ethnic and cultural backgrounds of participants in their programs than do schools or public sector service agencies, and to be *oriented to building on the strengths of families and youth rather than treating their deficits. Together these characteristics make their services both more accessible and supportive.* (19, emphasis mine)

The vision of incompetence is challenged both by the practices of the Beacons in building on the strengths of families rather than their deficits and by the outcome success of the Beacons in encouraging community participation, designing youth and adult programs, and delivering services. When staff at one Beacons program resisted the language of empowerment because it seemed to assume that the power wasn't already there in the community, they were expressing confidence in the community's ability, with adequate material resources, to foster relationships of mutual care.

The hesitance regarding the language of empowerment is warranted, for it often assumes that the population to be empowered is completely powerless. We should not, I think, allow ourselves to get caught in the trap of defining recipients as either powerful or powerless. This is far too unified a vision of the way power works and too homogeneous a vision of the powerless. While recipient populations in the context of traditional social services lack the power to influence the processes of institutional decision making regarding allocation of resources, they are not entirely resourceless. We might think, for example, about networks of shared norms, trust, and reciprocity as collective resources.[3] To acknowledge that these rela-

---

3. I am uncomfortable with the language of social capital as a way of understanding these networks because again it marks an attempt to treat relationships as commodities. But I introduce Putnam's argument regarding social capital here both because it is appropriate, given the argument I am making about the importance of community and relationships of trust, but also because many will recognize that Robert Putnam's *Making Democracy Work* (1993) raises questions about how we move from a situation in which democracy is not working to a situation in which it is. His case is very different — he is attempting to explain the fact that local regional governments in northern Italy are responsive democracies, while the same local governments in southern Italy are not — but I think it is instructive. He argues that it is the presence of social capital in northern Italy and its relative absence in southern Italy that accounts for this. But in trying to explain the presence or absence of social capital as a resource for democracy, Putnam relies on a very brief thousand-year overview of Italian history. His path dependency argument seems to amount to "you get social capital where you already have social capital." As Putnam himself realizes, this doesn't leave a lot of room for

tionships exist in the community is not to say, then, that all members of the community always get along.⁴ Rather, it is to say that there is some shared awareness of what is customary and some recognized mutual need to rely on one another. To survive at the socioeconomic margins requires informal networks, networks of child care, other-mothering, sharing vehicles, loaning money.⁵ These practices exist, not as contractual relationships between autonomous parties interested in rational exchange, but within the context of the relationships of care. Community-based organizations are at an advantage over more traditional social service bureaucracies because their place in the community, their history in the community, and the relationships of trust that are a product of this history, usually facilitate an awareness of these informal networks. Building on and fostering such networks is a critical part of the Beacons agenda. It is this ability to recognize the strengths and resources within the community that allows the Beacons to move away from a paternalistic model of care. In this sense, the Beacons programs are a model of more mutual care even in the larger context of often dramatic socioeconomic inequality.

The Beacons programs suggest that we can construct a model of public care in which (1) a more egalitarian distribution of material resources is accomplished through reallocation via our public institutions (here the dollars received from the city of New York's "Safe Streets, Safe Cities" fund), and (2) it is not assumed that those unable to meet their own material

---

optimism about the prospects for southern Italy's democracies. The project of cultivating social capital, I would argue, requires a shift in emphasis so that we not focus so heavily on its relative absence, but on locating and fostering it where it is present. Social capital can be "grown" where there is very little, but those interested in fostering it are always better to identify what there is and work from there. John McKnight (1995) refers to the need to map the strengths rather than the weaknesses of a community.

4. For a similar discussion, see Bernard Yack's *The Problems of a Political Animal* (1993) and Susan Bickford's response in *The Dissonance of Democracy* (1996, esp. 36–40). Yack offers an account of Aristotle's community in which friendship is understood as a minimal level of mutual concern rather than a thicker sense of shared virtue; communities here can be sites of dissonance, not merely accord.

5. For an excellent discussion of the power of these networks to provide for those at the margins, see Carol Stack's *All Our Kin* (1975). Also see Cheryl Townsend Gilkes's piece in *Women and the Politics of Empowerment* (1988). Melvin Delgado (1992) documents, for example, four types of "natural support systems" in Puerto Rican communities. *Natural* is used here explicitly to differentiate such systems from the professional caregiving systems of the community. They include family and friendship groups, local informal caregiving professionals, and mutual help groups. He argues that where schools and human service agencies ignore natural support systems, this manifests itself in policies and services that do not take into consideration cultural strengths and may even undermine these strengths (2).

needs in the marketplace are also unable to be democratic citizens. This model recognizes inequalities and differences in institutional power and suggests that the powerlessness of the "dependent" is not complete. A failure to recognize and build on the strengths that exist in these communities will produce paternalistic models of care. If policy works to identify networks of interdependence among those without institutional power and then supplies material resources to these networks, empowerment and more mutual relations of care can occur simultaneously.

A democratic politics of care moves a step beyond a democratic politics of needs interpretation because it assumes that equal membership in a democratic community requires an egalitarian distribution of the work of caretaking. What does this mean in practice? It means moving away from an institutionalized class of providers and an alternative class of recipients. The fluidity of these positions is critical to avoiding the institutionalization of paternalistic care. Because being in need is recognized as a social position rather than as a character trait — and because social positions can be fluid — a person who is at one point in need may at another point be capable of providing care. The alternative to paternalistic care becomes more mutual relationships of caretaking.

This commitment to mutuality must be reflected in program design at the outset. Beginning with a process of mapping community strengths and continuing with participant program planning sets the tone, but even the process of evaluation must reflect this commitment to mutual care in the context of a deliberative democratic community. Such a move would challenge both traditional forms of program evaluation and traditional conceptions of accountability. As an alternative, DeLysa Burnier has argued for "program evaluation as local knowledge," for a critical ethnographic approach to program evaluation. She argues that "where conventional program evaluation tends to focus mostly on outcomes, community-based programs require an evaluation approach that takes into account both process and outcome" (1999, 2). She builds on the work of Norman Denzin, describing a process of evaluation in which "a personally involved, politically committed [evaluator] is presumed and not the morally neutral observer" of traditional models of evaluation.[6] Burnier continues:

> Accordingly, the critical, interpretive ethnographic evaluator also would be expected to attend to the power inequalities that stand as

6. Denzin 1997, cited in Burnier 1999, 20.

obstructions to genuine empowerment. Additionally, the evaluator should be conscious of how his or her work could contribute to the goal of achieving community, and even structural change. . . .

Besides being committed to a set of values, a critical interpretive ethnographer tries to avoid "speaking for" or "on behalf" of CBDO [community-based development organizations] individuals and program participants. This objective is accomplished partially by levelling the hierarchy implied in the role of "outside expert," and instead working collaboratively with involved individuals by viewing them as co-researchers. . . . Further, the evaluator can escape the problem of "speaking for" the participants by making the project dialogical. This means that the evaluator and the participants examine and critique each other's organizational and program understandings, and both parties must be willing to change in light of the dialogical encounters (Gitlin, Siegel, Boru, 1989).

Such an approach resonates well with the commitments of a democratic politics of care. When New Futures completed its evaluation and summed up its "lessons learned," it focused on a failure to meet outcome goals and attributed this to a lack of adequate expert planning. Burnier's alternative model acknowledges the importance of process and contests the conventional understanding of expertise. Both are critical components of a democratic politics of care.

The Contestability of Needs

I have focused throughout this project on the process of interpreting needs. As a consequence, it makes sense that as I refine my framework for a democratic politics of care, I draw on deliberative theories of democracy. But I want to acknowledge that this focus on interpretation is at odds with much of the current work on needs. I recognize that many of those concerned with meeting needs, particularly needs understood as basic — food, shelter, clothing — are uncomfortable with this focus. Can we not say with some conviction that no matter what the politics of interpretation surrounding needs, these needs are "real" in a way that the need for a cellular phone is not? And if we were to argue the contrary case, wouldn't we just be getting needs "wrong"?

We must begin with the recognition that the claim that some needs are "real" is not an immediately political one. To become political, it must entail a call to act, presumably to meet these "real" needs. Where this claim is made in order to prompt political action, say a more equitable distribution of resources, I have sympathies with the motives of proponents. But the difficulties of actually distributing resources more equitably remain largely unaddressed when we claim that some needs are "real." Given that there are many in our society whose "real" needs go unmet, the political project must begin with the assumption that the general public is either unpersuaded by the assertion that there are "real" needs, or is persuaded by it in theory but not in practice—that is, they are persuaded of the ontological claim, but it doesn't translate into a clear agenda for political practice. Where someone is unpersuaded by the claim that the need for shelter, food, and clothing is "real," the process of persuasion must begin with an inquiry into their alternative interpretation of need.

Where someone is convinced in theory but not in practice, we must ask questions about the institutional structures that make meeting the "real" needs of some so difficult. I have argued that this process of inquiry, as well as any deliberation about institutional reorganization, should be situated in a democratic context. Deliberation matters because needs are contested, because there are differing interpretations of need—such differences are what make democracy necessary. Again, as Anne Phillips suggests, while there is no guarantee that consensus will be the product of such deliberations, there is at least an increased hope of the mutual understanding necessary for collective action.

Is it helpful, then, to talk about people getting their own needs *wrong?* If so, and if we are committed to democratic deliberation, do we have to "let them be wrong"? There is no doubt that the process of deliberation is in part to be valued because it is a learning process, but such a claim entails several assumptions that I think we must reject. First, it assumes that we can separate process from outcome and that we can know in advance of a democratic process what the right outcome is. In short, the claim that democrats have to let those who deliberate be wrong seems to assume that those who judge the deliberative interpretation of need stand outside the deliberative process and are in the position of "the idealized paternalist." I have already suggested that I find such a notion problematic because it seems to assume the possibility of perfect information based on a hypothetical condition, while those who would make actual knowledge claims are actual persons with necessarily limited understandings. It also assumes that the deliberative process is somehow irrelevant.

Perhaps the best demonstration of the importance of process is the interview with a street outreach coordinator who said not only that it is important for the community to do its own needs assessment but also that community members shouldn't tell other community members, "This is what you need." Rather, he says, "You go up to them and you ask them what they need"—you begin a dialogue. And then he added, "You don't ask people, 'Do you need a job?' You ask people what they need, and you let them tell you they need a job." It was clear he had thought a lot about needs assessment as a process that should invite dialogue, that should avoid assuming the needs of people in advance of such a dialogue. The inseparability of such a dialogical process from an appropriate understanding of needs is clear.

The process of interpreting needs is important for another reason: it is important to getting a more complete understanding of needs. Needs themselves are rarely needs for simple "things." In fact, needs are most often bound up with our social relationships. This is what makes it difficult to talk about either needs or care as commodities. When the provider of care intervenes, which is after all the politically meaningful consequence of knowing needs, the provider/paternalist has an actual identity that is, as we have seen, relevant to how successful intervention or care will be. In this sense, meeting needs, providing care, is a social process in which the identities of those involved matters very much.

While it may be philosophically satisfying to delineate a theory of human need, actually satisfying those needs—in Tronto's words, "getting the work of care done"—depends on a process of political persuasion and institutional reorganization. Divorced from such contextual concerns, claims about "real" needs seem irrelevant for political practice. Thinking about needs as embedded within a sociopolitical context makes for messy theories of need. But a theory of need that begins with the recognition that in practice needs *are* contested is more apt as a guide for politics.

Democracy and Disagreement

Having said this, then what are we to do when in the course of deliberation we are unable to reach consensus on what needs should have priority and how they should be met? I have suggested that community-based organizations can be important to the process of public care because they can facilitate relationships of mutual care, care more appropriate to a democratic context than the paternalistic care produced in a more bureaucratic model. But such organizations are important to a democratic politics of care for a second set of reasons as well.

The deliberative model I am suggesting recognizes contestation. It also recognizes that action resolves that contestation in favor of some but not all participants of the dialogue. Jane Mansbridge suggests that such moments are necessarily coercive moments in the course of deliberative democracy:

> Good deliberation will have opened areas of agreement and will have clarified the remaining areas of conflict. The participants will have come to understand their interests, including their conflicting interests better than before deliberation. But material interests and interests in one's deepest values, cannot always be reconciled with the interests, material and ideal of others. At this point when conflict remains after good deliberation, a democracy has two choices, to remain at the status quo or to act by coercing some to go along with others. (1996, 47)

Coercion of some participants is necessary in any case where there is not consensus; if we are to act, we are to act because we are willing to "coerce" those who have not been persuaded yet.

Mansbridge does not argue that majority rule can legitimate this coercion: "[N]o coercion can be either incontestably fair or predictably just." In light of this, "democracies must find ways of fighting while they use it, the very coercion that they need" (47). Mansbridge argues that an important institutional safeguard against coercive power is what she calls "informal deliberative enclaves of resistance," or what Fraser (1992) has called "subaltern counterpublics." In the context of these groups, those who lose in each coercive move can rework their ideas and their strategies, gathering their forces and deciding in a more protected space in what way or whether to continue the battle (47). Such groups can formulate oppositional interpretations of their identities, interests, and needs.

This does not rid us of the "ongoing imperfection of democratic decision," as Mansbridge understands it. Actual democracies are always at best a "rough" or "good enough" approximation of political equality, for example. Mansbridge argues that people's willingness to accept some coercion as "legitimate enough" is seldom a result of an "explicit or reflectively achieved consensus formed by unconstrained discussion. That willingness derives largely from a conventional and unreflective consensus rooted in the internalization of social and cultural traditions" (55). So coercion is never perfectly legitimate.

If we are to fight the coercive power of democracies at the same time as we use it, democracies must multiply the deliberative arenas available, create the space for—and, I have argued, even support with material resources—community organizations that might be considered "counterpublics." This, Mansbridge argues, will facilitate critiques of power from different directions; and revealing coercive power is certainly necessary, if not sufficient, to fighting it.

It would be naive to legitimate deliberative processes with an argument that such processes are the best way to achieve consensus. As Benjamin Barber (1983) and more recently Susan Bickford (1996) have both argued, deliberative democracy is to be valued for the way it handles conflict, but "handling" conflict does not eliminate dissonance. What it does do is begin to remedy the problem of "underdescription" that Friedman (1993) alluded to, to make possible "mutual understanding," if not "mutual agreement."

As Anne Phillips (1995) suggests, we get better at understanding the situations of others when the "other" has been well represented. Community-based deliberation provides the best opportunities for such representation.

Pathology and Parochialism

At this point I have, I hope, offered a loose framework for public care that avoids the problem of paternalism and thus is more appropriate to a democratic context. Yet Joan Tronto suggested that paternalism was one of a twin set of concerns: the other is the problem of parochialism. That is, if we accept a model of public care premised in an assumption of interdependence, recognizing the possibility and desirability of mutual care within a democratic context, how do we ensure that our "circles of care" are not inappropriately exclusionary? I have referred throughout this project to "communities." How are these communities defined? Who is a member and how is this determined?

This question can not be answered in the abstract. In reviewing the work of Nel Noddings, I was critical of her assumption that "circles of care" are derivative of natural affective ties. I argued instead that such circles are the product of social and political practices. On this account, we confront the process of circumscribing circles of care as a political process. Within the framework I am proposing, the problem of parochialism may be understood as a problem of constructing the boundaries of community. And given that they are constructed, they can be reconstructed.

The case studies in Chapter 2 demonstrated that the historical practices of providers often created community boundaries by creating a sense of "us versus them" in the communities of designated "at risk." Even the process of establishing the "target population" for New Futures implied pathology. Although the traditional approach to research treats the target population as a discovery, as Anne Schneider and Helen Ingram have suggested,

> the social construction of target populations is an important, albeit overlooked, political phenomenon that should take its place in the study of public policy by political scientists.
>
> The social construction of target populations refers to the cultural characterizations or popular images of the persons or groups whose behavior and well-being is affected by public policy. These characterizations are normative and evaluative, portraying groups in positive or negative terms through symbolic language, metaphors, and stories (Edelman 1964, 1988). (1993, 334)

The construction of the target population for New Futures was geographical, determined by high rates of crime, dilapidated housing, and teen pregnancy. The map portrayed the community in terms of its incompetencies rather than its competencies. In light of this, it should not be surprising that, despite initial commitments to the contrary, it was difficult for collaborative members to take community members seriously as equal participants in decision making.

This tendency to pathologize recipients of traditional social services was well recognized among Beacons staffers. Their vision of their community rejected such a portrait, emphasizing the ways in which their community was "not that different from any other," with resources as well as needs. Their vision of the community prompts a reconsideration of the construction of target communities. This process, staffers argued, must involve the community in doing its own needs assessment. We might add that the community must simultaneously assess its own resources. What networks for caretaking, formal or informal, are in place already? Which organizations in the community have the capacity to orchestrate a reorganization of public care? Who might be appropriate for doing needs assessment? What does the map of community strengths look like?

This suggests that the picture of a community designated "at risk" might be constructed very differently. But could we reconstruct the boundaries of the community more inclusively? This seems to be the primary concern raised in the charge of parochialism. Again, the question cannot be answered in the abstract. In the immediate run, a sense of distrust toward outsiders—distrust based in an extended history of failed commitments to care, whether malicious or merely inept—seems to be a barrier to expanding the boundaries of the communities presented in the case studies. This distrust is neither natural nor inevitable; it is not a consequence of some innate sense that we have about "caring for our own." We can both trust and care for those very different from ourselves, but where difference intersects with radical inequality, neither is likely. Yet because this inequality and the distrust it tends to produce are products of institutional practices, the reconstruction of institutions might, over time, produce the minimal levels of trust necessary to constructing a more inclusive deliberative community.

The problem of parochialism is revealing, for it is not typically the parochialism of communities "at risk" about which we are concerned. When Tronto, for example, illustrates the potential problem of parochialism within a care framework, she suggests: "If those who are the most wealthy and powerful are allowed simply to pay special attention to their own needs because those are the ones that they are closest to and most well acquainted with, the problems of unequal resource distribution could actually be justified rather than overturned by the focus on care" (1996, 148). More often than not, we are concerned that those who live in communities with a disproportionate share of material resources will be parochial. We are worried because such practices of care would, as Tronto suggests, perpetuate inequalities of which we want to be critical. But is parochialism itself a problem, or is it the parochialism of the powerful in particular that we want to criticize?

The turn to justice would seem to suggest that it is all parochialisms that are a problem. Conceptually, justice, with its commitment to impartiality and universality, would seem to provide the necessary bulwark against parochialism. Yet from the perspective of deliberative democracy as Mansbridge understands it, it seems that not all parochialisms are equal; some have a critical role to play in maintaining deliberative spaces to supplement and challenge the formal deliberative processes that take place in local and national governments. She remarks, "The present reigning hostility to 'identity politics' does not recognize the value to democracy of deliberative enclaves in which the relatively like-minded can consult easily with one another" (1996, 57). The examples Mansbridge uses include working-class citizens, black colleges, and women's consciousness raising groups. Such groups were often as important for the mutual support that they provided as for the opportunity to strategize about politics. But the fact that her examples all involve groups that have traditionally been disenfranchised suggests that some parochialism may be necessary in order to create the space to redress historical exclusions. She continues: "Much contemporary work on civil society recognizes how partial, conflicting deliberative spaces, which yield partial and conflicting accounts of self-interest as well as conflicting accounts of the common good, must supplement both mainstream discourse about the common good and the formal deliberations that take place in local and national governments" (57). Thus community-based organizations are vital to a democratic politics of care both because they are better able to identify and foster the networks of informal care that are the basis of mutual care, and because they are critical to a democratic process of needs interpretation within the immediate community and beyond it.

Deliberative democracy of the kind I have been discussing, equal voice and equal consideration, is difficult; and it is made more difficult in the context of radical material inequality. For ultimately it is this material inequality, its convergence with race and ethnicity, that constructs the situation one case manager described as "two different worlds, speaking two different languages." Yet these worlds often collide, providing moments where we can see the connections.

Why should those beyond the community commit material resources to provide care within it? The director of one New Futures program tried to persuade local businesses that they would "pay now or pay later" — it was funding for youth programs now or funding for prisons later. It was a strategy that worked to keep businesses involved; and while the message seems dire, it gets to an important truth. Those worlds may be different, but they are not totally isolated from one another. As New Futures illustrates, across this divide translations evolve into "misunderstandings" and manipulations; deliberation is difficult both to initiate and to maintain.

The hope, I think, is not for perfect communication or flawless translation, for this, like impartiality, is impossible to achieve. "Mutual understanding" involves negotiating partialities, confessing and interrogating our parochialism, and confronting the institutional organizations, both formal and informal, that maintain inequality across difference. If democratic empowerment means anything, it must mean a citizenry empowered to deliberate. Public care appropriate to a democratic state requires the same commitment to deliberation — deliberation in which everyone engaged in the process of care has a voice that is heard.

References

Alcoff, Linda. 1991. "The Problem of Speaking for Others." *Cultural Critique* (Winter).

Alcoff, Linda, and Elizabeth Porter, eds. 1993. *Feminist Epistemologies*. New York: Routledge.

Annie E. Casey Foundation. 1988. *A Strategic Planning Guide for the New Future Initiative*. Greenwich, Conn.: Annie E. Casey Foundation.

Baier, Annette. 1985. *Postures of the Mind: Essays on Mind and Morals*. Minneapolis: University of Minnesota Press.

———. 1987. "Hume, the Women's Moral Theorist?" In *Women and Moral Theory*, ed. Eva Kittay and Diana Meyers. Savage, Md.: Rowman and Littlefield.

———. 1990. *A Progress of Sentiments*. Cambridge: Harvard University Press.

Barber, Bernard. 1983. *The Logic and Limits of Trust*. New Brunswick: Rutgers University Press.

———. 1984. *Strong Democracy*. Berkeley and Los Angeles: University of California Press.

Benhabib, Seyla. 1987. "The Generalized and the Concrete Other: The Kohlberg-Gilligan Controversy and Moral Theory." In *Women and Moral Theory*, ed. Eva Kittay and Diana Meyers. Savage, Md.: Rowman and Littlefield.

———. 1996. "Toward a Deliberative Model of Democratic Legitimacy." In *Democracy and Difference: Contesting the Boundaries of the Political*, ed. Seyla Benhabib. Princeton: Princeton University Press.

Berger, David. 1984. "On the Way to Empathic Understanding." *American Journal of Psychotherapy* (January).

Bickford, Susan. 1996. *The Dissonance of Democracy: Listening, Conflict, and Citizenship*. Ithaca: Cornell University Press.

Blum, Lawrence. 1980. *Friendship, Altruism, and Morality*. Boston: Routledge.

———. 1987. "Gilligan and Kohlberg: Implications for Moral Theory." In *Women and Moral Theory*, ed. Eva Kittay and Diana Meyers. Savage, Md.: Rowman and Littlefield.

Bowles, Samuel, and Herbert Gintis. 1976. *Schooling in Capitalist America*. New York: Basic Books.

Brager, George. 1965. "The Indigenous Worker: A New Approach to the Social Work Technician." *Social Work* (April).

Bubeck, Diemut. 1995. *Care, Gender, and Justice*. Oxford: Oxford University Press.

Buchanan, Allen. 1983. "Medical Paternalism." In *Paternalism*, ed. Rolf Sartorius. Minneapolis: University of Minnesota Press.

Burnier, DeLysa. 1999. "Program Evaluation as Local Knowledge: Towards a Critical Ethnographic Approach." Paper presented for Midwest Political Science Association, April.

Butler, Melissa. [1978] 1995. "Early Liberal Roots of Feminism: John Locke and the Attack on Patriarchy." In *Feminism and Philosophy: Essential Readings in Theory, Reinterpretation, and Application,* ed. Nancy Tuana and Rosemary Tong. Boulder: Westview Press.

Cahill, Michelle, et al. 1993. *A Documentation Report on the New York City Beacons Initiative.* New York: The Youth Development Institute, December.

Calhoun, Cheshire, and Robert Solomon. 1984. *What Is an Emotion? Classical Readings in Philosophical Psychology.* New York: Oxford University Press.

Card, Claudia. 1990. "Caring and Evil." *Hypatia* (Spring).

Center for the Study of Social Policy. 1995. *New Futures: Results of a Groundbreaking Social Experiment in Five Cities.* Washington, D.C.: Center for the Study of Social Policy.

Chambliss, Daniel F. 1996. *Beyond Caring: Hospitals, Nurses, and the Social Organization of Care Ethics.* Chicago: University of Chicago Press.

Code, Lorraine. 1987. *Epistemic Responsibility.* Hanover: Brown University Press.

———. 1991. *What Can One Know? Feminist Theory and the Construction of Knowledge.* Ithaca: Cornell University Press.

———. 1993. "Taking Subjectivity into Account." In *Feminist Epistemologies,* ed. Linda Alcoff and Elizabeth Porter. New York: Routledge.

———. 1995. *Rhetorical Spaces.* New York: Routledge.

Cremin, Lawrence. 1961. *The Transformation of the School.* New York: Vintage Books.

Cudaback, Dorothea. 1969. "Case-Sharing in the AFDC Program: The Use of Welfare Service Aides." *Social Work* (July).

Davies, Gareth. 1992. "War on Dependency: Liberal Individualism and the Economic Opportunity Act of 1964." *Journal of American Studies* 26, no. 2.

Delgado, Melvin. 1992. *The Puerto Rican Community and Natural Support Systems: Implications for the Education of Children.* Boston: Center on Families, Communities, Schools, and Children's Learning.

Dempsey, Van, and George Noblit. 1996. "Caring and Continuity: The Demise of Caring in an African-American Community: One Consequence of School Desegregation." In *Caring in an Unjust World: Negotiating Borders and Barriers in Schools,* ed. Deborah Eaker-Rich and Jan VanGalen. Albany: SUNY Press.

Denzin, Norman. 1997. *Interpretive Ethnography: Ethnographic Practices for the 21st Century.* Thousand Oaks, Calif.: Sage.

Deutsch, Francine, and Ronald Madle. 1975. "Empathy: Historic and Current Conceptualizations, Measurement, and a Cognitive Theoretical Perspective." *Human Development* 18.

Dworkin, Gerald. 1983a. "Paternalism." In *Paternalism,* ed. Rolf Sartorius. Minneapolis: University of Minnesota.

———. 1983b. "Paternalism: Some Second Thoughts." In *Paternalism,* ed. Rolf Sartorius. Minneapolis: University of Minnesota.

Elster, Jon. 1986. "The Market and the Forum: Three Varieties of Political Theory." In *Foundations of Social Choice Theory,* ed. Aanund Hylland and John Elster. Cambridge: Cambridge University Press.

Ferguson, Kathy E. 1984. *The Feminist Case Against Bureaucracy.* Philadelphia: Temple University Press.

Flanagan, Owen, and Amelie Rorty, eds. 1990. *Identity, Character, and Morality.* Cambridge: MIT Press.

Flax, Jane. 1978. "The Conflict Between Nurturance and Autonomy in Mother-Daughter Relationships and Within Feminism." *Feminist Studies* 4, no. 2.

Fraser, Nancy. 1989. *Unruly Practices: Power, Discourse, and Gender in Contemporary Social Theory*. Minneapolis: University of Minnesota Press.

———. 1990. "Struggle Over Needs: Outline of a Socialist-Feminist Critical Theory of Late-Capitalist Political Culture." In *Women, the State, and Welfare*, ed. Linda Gordon, 199–226. Madison: University of Wisconsin.

———. 1992. "Rethinking the Public Sphere: A Contribution to the Critique of Actually Existing Democracy." In *Habermas and the Public Sphere*, ed. Craig Calhoun. Cambridge: MIT Press.

Fraser, Nancy, and Linda Gordon. 1994. "Dependency: A Keyword of the Welfare State." *Signs* (Winter).

———. 1997. "Decoding 'Dependency': Inscriptions of Power in a Keyword of the U.S. Welfare State." In *Reconstructing Political Theory: Feminist Perspectives*, ed. Mary Lyndon Shanley and Uma Narayan. University Park: Pennsylvania State University Press.

Friedman, Marilyn. 1993. *What Are Friends For? Feminist Perspectives on Personal Relationships and Moral Theory*. Ithaca: Cornell University Press.

Gatens, Moira. 1991. *Feminism and Philosophy: Perspectives on Difference and Equality*. Bloomington: Indiana University Press.

Gaylin, Willard, et al., eds. 1981. *Doing Good: The Limits of Benevolence*. New York: Pantheon Books.

Gilkes, Cheryl Townsend. 1988. "Building in Many Places: Multiple Commitments and Ideologies in Black Women's Community Work." In *Women and the Politics of Empowerment*, ed. Ann Bookman and Sandra Morgen. Philadelphia: Temple University Press.

Gilligan, Carol. [1982] 1993. *In a Different Voice*. Cambridge: Harvard University Press.

———. 1987. "Moral Orientation and Moral Development." In *Women and Moral Theory*, ed. Eva Kittay and Diana Meyers. Savage, Md.: Rowman and Littlefield.

———. 1988. "Exit-Voice Dilemmas." In *Mapping the Moral Domain*, ed. Carol Gilligan, Carol Ward, Victoria Taylor, and Jill McClean. Cambridge: Harvard University Press.

Gilliom, John. 1998. "Welfare Surveillance, Rights, and the Politics of Care: A Case Study of (Non)Legal (Non)Mobilization." Paper prepared for the Western Political Science Association, March.

Gingrich, Newt. 1994. *Contract with America*. New York: Times Books.

Glendon, Mary Ann. 1991. *Rights Talk: The Impoverishment of Political Discourse*. New York: Free Press.

Gordon, Linda, ed. 1990. *Women, the State, and Welfare*. Madison: University of Wisconsin Press.

Govier, Trudy. 1992. "Trust, Distrust, and Feminist Theory." *Hypatia* (Winter).

Handler, Joel. 1996. *Down from Bureaucracy*. Princeton: Princeton University Press.

Hardcastle, David A. 1971. "The Indigenous Nonprofessional in the Social Service Bureaucracy: A Critical Examination." *Social Work* (April).

Hart, Vivien. 1978. *Distrust and Democracy*. Cambridge: Cambridge University Press.

Held, Virginia. 1984. *Rights and Goods*. New York: Free Press.

———. 1995. "Introduction." In her *Justice and Care: Essential Readings in Feminist Ethics*. Boulder: Westview Press.

Hill, Thomas. 1987. "The Importance of Autonomy." In *Women and Moral Theory,* ed. Eva Kittay and Diana Meyers. Savage, Md.: Rowman and Littlefield.

Hirschmann, Nancy. 1992. *Rethinking Obligation: A Feminist Method for Political Theory.* Ithaca: Cornell University Press.

———. 1996. "Toward a Feminist Theory of Freedom." *Political Theory* 24, no. 1 (February).

Hoagland, Sarah Lucia. 1990. "Some Concerns About Nel Noddings: 'Caring.'" *Hypatia* (Spring).

Honig, Bonnie. 1993. *Political Theory and the Displacement of Politics.* Ithaca: Cornell University Press.

Hume, David. 1948. *Moral and Political Philosophy,* ed. Henry D. Aiken. New York: Hafner Press.

Jones, Kathleen. 1993. *Compassionate Authority: Democracy and the Representation of Women.* New York: Routledge.

Kant, Immanuel. [1797] 1987. *The Metaphysical Elements of Justice.* New York: Macmillan.

Katz, Michael. 1977. *Class, Bureaucracy, and Schools.* New York: Praeger.

Kauffman-Osborne, Timothy. 1993. "Teasing Feminist Sense from Experience." *Hypatia* (Spring).

Kiss, Elizabeth. 1997. "Alchemy or Fool's Gold: Assessing Feminist Doubts About Rights." In *Reconstructing Political Theory: Feminist Perspectives,* ed. Mary Lyndon Shanley and Uma Narayan. University Park: Pennsylvania State University Press.

Kittay, Eva, and Meyers, Diana. 1987. "Introduction." In *Women and Moral Theory,* ed. Eva Kittay and Diana Meyers. Savage, Md.: Rowman and Littlefield.

Kohlberg, Lawrence, and Carol Gilligan. 1971. "The Adolescent as a Philosopher: The Discovery of the Self in a Postconventional World." *Daedalus* 100:1051–86.

Kohlberg, Lawrence, and R. Kramer. 1969. "Continuities and Discontinuities in Childhood and Adult Moral Development." *Human Development* (December).

Larrabee, Mary Jeanne. 1993. "Gender and Moral Development: A Challenge for Feminist Theory." In *An Ethic of Care: Feminist and Interdisciplinary Perspectives,* ed. Mary Larrabee. London: Routledge.

Locke, John. [1690] 1994. *Two Treatises on Government.* New York: Cambridge University Press.

Loewenberg, Frank M. 1968. "Social Workers and Indigenous Nonprofessionals: Some Structural Dilemmas." *Social Work* (July).

Lyons, Nona. 1983. "Two Perspectives: On Self, Relationships, and Morality." *Harvard Educational Review* (May).

Mansbridge, Jane. 1992. "A Deliberative Theory of Interest Representation." In *The Politics of Interests,* ed. Mark P. Petracca. Boulder: Westview Press.

———. 1996. "Using Power/Fighting Power: The Polity." In *Democracy and Difference: Contesting the Boundaries of the Political,* ed. Seyla Benhabib. Princeton: Princeton University Press.

Martin, Elaine. 1986. "Consumer Evaluation of Human Services." *Social Policy and Administration* 20, no. 3 (Autumn).

McKnight, John. 1995. *The Careless Society: Community and Its Counterfeits.* New York: Basic Books.

Michaels, Meredith. 1986. "Morality Without Distinction." *The Philosophical Forum* (Spring).
Mill, John Stuart. [1859] 1956. *On Liberty.* New York: Liberal Arts Press.
Mills, Charles. 1997. *The Racial Contract.* Ithaca: Cornell University Press.
Mitchell, Lawrence. 1998. *Stacked Deck: A Story of Selfishness in America.* Philadelphia: Temple University Press.
Nicholson, Linda. 1986. *Gender and History: The Limits of Social Theory in the Age of the Family.* New York: Columbia University Press.
———. 1993. "Women, Morality, and History." In *An Ethic of Care,* ed. Mary Larrabee. New York: Routledge.
Noddings, Nel. 1984. *Caring: A Feminine Approach to Ethics.* Berkeley: University of California Press.
Okin, Susan. 1990. "Reason and Feeling in Thinking About Justice." In *Feminism and Political Theory,* ed. Cass R. Sunstein. Chicago: University of Chicago Press.
Pateman, Carole. 1988. *The Sexual Contract.* Oxford: Polity Press.
———. 1989. *The Disorder of Women.* Stanford: Stanford University Press.
Phillips, Anne. 1993. *Democracy and Difference.* University Park: Pennsylvania State University Press.
———. 1995. *The Politics of Presence.* Oxford: Clarendon Press.
Putnam, Robert. 1993. *Making Democracy Work: Civic Traditions in Modern Italy.* Princeton: Princeton University Press, 1993.
Rawls, John. 1971. *A Theory of Justice.* Cambridge: Harvard University Press.
Regan, Donald. 1974. "Justifications for Paternalism." In *The Limits of Law,* ed. J. Roland Pennock and John W. Chapman. New York: Liever and Atherton.
———. 1983. "Paternalism, Freedom, Identity, and Commitment." In *Paternalism,* ed. Rolf Sartorius. Minneapolis: University of Minnesota Press.
Rooney, Phyllis. 1993. "Feminist-Pragmatist Revisionings of Reason, Knowledge, Philosophy." *Hypatia* (Spring).
Rothman, David J. 1981. "The State as Parent: Social Policy in the Progressive Era." In *Doing Good,* ed. Willard Gaylin et al. New York: Pantheon Books.
Sanders, Lynn. 1997. "Against Deliberation." *Political Theory* 25(3): 347–76.
Sartorius, Rolf, ed. 1983. *Paternalism.* Minneapolis: University of Minnesota Press.
Schneider, Anne, and Helen Ingram. 1993. "Social Construction of Target Populations: Implications for Politics and Policy." *American Political Science Review* (June).
Sennett, Richard. 1980. *Authority.* New York: Random House.
Sevenhuijsen, Selma. 1998. *Citizenship and the Ethics of Care: Feminist Considerations on Justice, Morality, and Politics.* New York: Routledge.
Shklar, Judith. 1990. *Faces of Injustice.* New Haven: Yale University Press.
Showstack Sassoon, Anne, ed. 1987. *Women and the State.* London: Hutcheson.
Smiley, Marion. 1989. "Paternalism and Democracy." *Journal of Value Inquiry* 23 (December).
———. 1992. *Moral Responsibility and the Boundaries of Community.* Chicago: University of Chicago Press.
Solomon, Robert. 1990. *A Passion for Justice.* New York: Addison-Wesley.
Spragens, Thomas. 1981. *The Irony of Liberal Reason.* Chicago: University of Chicago Press.
Stack, Carol. 1975. *All Our Kin.* New York: Harper and Row.
Sunstein, Cass R., ed. 1990. *Feminism and Political Theory.* Chicago: University of Chicago Press.

Thomas, Lawrence. 1990. "Trust, Affirmation, and Moral Character: A Critique of Kantian Morality." In *Identity, Character, and Morality*, ed. Owen Flanagan and Amelie Rorty, 235–57. Cambridge: MIT Press.

Tronto, Joan. 1993. *Moral Boundaries: A Political Argument for an Ethic of Care*. New York: Routledge.

———. 1996. "Care as a Political Concept." In *Revisioning the Political: Feminist Reconstructions of Traditional Concepts in Western Political Theory*, ed. Nancy J. Hirschmann and Christine DiStefano. Boulder: Westview.

Tyack, David, and Elisabeth Hansot. 1982. *Managers of Virtue: Public School Leadership in America, 1820–1980*. New York: Basic Books.

VanGalen, Jan. 1996. "Caring in Community: The Limitations of Compassion in Facilitating Diversity." In *Caring in an Unjust World: Negotiating Borders and Barriers in Schools*, ed. Deborah Eaker-Rich and Jan VanGalen. Albany: SUNY Press.

Walker, Margaret Urban. 1989. "Moral Understandings: Alternative 'Epistemology' for a Feminist Ethics." *Hypatia* 4, no. 2 (Summer).

———. 1996. "Feminist Skepticism, Authority, and Transparency." In *Moral Knowledge: New Readings in Epistemology*, ed. Walter Sinnott-Armstrong and Mark Timmons. New York: Oxford University Press.

Whitman, David. 1992. "The Next War on Poverty: An Agenda for Change." *U.S. News & World Report* (October 5): 36–37.

Wispe, Lauren. 1986. "The Distinction Between Sympathy and Empathy: To Call Forth a Concept, a Word Is Needed." *Journal of Personality and Social Psychology* 50, no. 2.

Yack, Bernard. 1992. *The Longing for Total Revolution: Philosophic Sources of Social Discontent from Rousseau to Marx and Nietzsche*. Berkeley: University of California Press.

———. 1993. *The Problems of a Political Animal*. Berkeley: University of California Press.

Young, Iris Marion. 1986. "Impartiality and the Civic Public: Some Implications of Feminist Critiques of Moral and Political Theory." *Praxis International* 5 (January).

———. 1993. "Justice and Communicative Democracy." In *Radical Philosophy: Tradition, Counter Tradition, Politics*, ed. Roger S. Gottlieb. Philadelphia: Temple University Press.

———. 1996. "Communication and the Other: Beyond Deliberative Democracy." In *Democracy and Difference*, ed. Seyla Benhabib. Princeton: Princeton University Press.

Index

governance, practice of care and, 42–46
Govier, Trudy, 139
Guardians of Culture, 29–30, 80

Handler, Joel, 157–60
Hardcastle, David A., 41 n. 10
harm minimization principle, distribution of care and, 89–92
Held, Virginia, 63
Hill, Thomas, 64
Hirschmann, Albert, 78–79
Hirschmann, Nancy, 127 n. 2
Hoagland, Sarah, 114, 116
Honig, Bonnie, 14 n. 15, 63–67
Hume, David, 53, 62; ethics of care and, 79; moral obligation model, 65–68; politics and morality in, 62–63, 64 n. 8

identity: politics of needs determination and, 94–98; practice of care and, 137–43; Rawlsian justice, 108–9. *See also* ethnic identity; racial identity
ignorance, veil of: justice and, 48–52, 82 n. 3; politics of needs determination and, 94–98; Rawlsian view of justice and, 105–9, 107 n. 4
impartiality: deliberative democracy and, 148–52, 171–73; distribution of care and, 89–92; versus empathy, 102–3, 110–11; ethics of care and, 16, 53–54, 76–77; justice and, 108–9, 143–45
In a Different Voice, 53, 54–62, 77–80
inclusion: versus consensus, in New Futures project, 34; of recipients, in Beacons project, 43–46
individualism: liberal democratic equality and, 151 n. 14; politics of care and, 88; welfare policy and, 9–10
inequality. *See* equality
information gaps: empowerment and asymmetry in, 158–59; politics and, 22–24. *See also* communication gaps
Ingram, Helen, 36 n. 8, 170
interactive universalism, politics of needs determination and, 96–98
interdependence: mutual care relationships and, 160–65; politics of care and, 156–60
intervention, paternalism and, 11–15, 73–77, 127–31, 136–37, 139, 155

Jaggar, Alison, 106
job training programs, lack of consensus on, in New Futures project, 34
Johnson, Lyndon B., 9–10
Jones, Kathleen, 118–21, 137–38, 143, 149–50
judgment, care and empathy and, 115; character and, 139
justice: care as injustice, 52–54, 72–77; care as requirement for, 101–21, 154–55; democracy and, 98–100; ethics of care and, 48–52, 72; Gilligan's version of, 77–80; Noddings on care without, 81–87; parochialism and, 171–73; paternalism and, 73–77; racism and sexism and, 75; social contract theory and, 109–11; Solomon's theory of, 112–15; stage theory of moral development and, 57–62. *See also* distributive justice

Kant, Immanuel, 53, 62–66; Okin on influence of Kant on Rawls, 105–9; paternalism and, 126
Kaufman-Osborne, Timothy, 119
Kittay, Eva, 51, 53
knowledge: contractarian vision of empathy and caring, 103–5; empathy and justice and model for, 111–21; ethics of care and politics of need and, 68–70; idealization of paternalism and, 129–31; neutrality claims and power of, 120–21; politics of, in New Futures project, 25–30
Kohlberg, Lawrence: on Kant's theory of justice, 66, 106–7; moral development stages of, 52–62, 69, 77–81, 103 n. 1; on paternalism, 127; politics of needs determination and, 94, 97–98
Kramer, R., 60

language: of empowerment, democratization of care and, 162–65; Gilligan's ethic of care and, 78–80; pathologization of communities and, 36–37
liberal democracy: autonomy and care in, 2–3; deliberative model of, 146; empathy and epistemology in, 111–15; paternalism and, 13–15; practice of care and needs definition, 45–46; self-sufficiency and, 9–11; theory of justice and, 51, 53–54, 150 n. 13; utilitarianism and, 127–31